ADORABLE
BABY CROCHET

ADORABLE
BABY CROCHET

Kristi Simpson

STACKPOLE
BOOKS

Guilford, Connecticut

Published by Stackpole Books
An imprint of The Rowman & Littlefield Publishing Group, Inc.
4501 Forbes Blvd., Ste. 200
Lanham, MD 20706
www.stackpolebooks.com

Distributed by NATIONAL BOOK NETWORK
800-462-6420

Model/project photography by Backroad Photography by Jenn
Technique photography by Kristi Simpson

British Library Cataloguing in Publication Information available

Library of Congress Cataloging-in-Publication Data available

Names: Simpson, Kristi, author.
Title: Adorable baby crochet / Kristi Simpson.
Description: First edition. | Lanham : Stackpole Books, an imprint of
  Rowman & Littlefield Publishing Group, Inc., 2020. | Includes index. |
  Summary: "Babies are adorable, and their crocheted swag should be, too!
  Sizes from newborn to 12 months will keep baby in style for their first
  year, and toys and blankets will continue to bring joy for years to
  come!"— Provided by publisher.
Identifiers: LCCN 2019038526 (print) | LCCN 2019038527 (ebook) | ISBN
  9780811738385 (paperback) | ISBN 9780811768382 (epub)
Subjects: LCSH: Crocheting—Patterns. | Infants' clothing.
Classification: LCC TT825 .S54627 2020 (print) | LCC TT825 (ebook) | DDC
  746.43/4—dc23
LC record available at https://lccn.loc.gov/2019038526
LC ebook record available at https://lccn.loc.gov/2019038527

♾™ The paper used in this publication meets the minimum requirements of
American National Standard for Information Sciences—Permanence of Paper for
Printed Library Materials, ANSI/NISO Z39.48-1992.

First Edition

Contents

Introduction

These forty-plus patterns are perfect if you want to create something special for the new or growing baby in your life. And you know that when it comes to crocheting for babies, it has to be *adorable*! Whether you're looking for patterns for a newborn or older baby, the patterns in this book are quick to make and sure to please babies and moms alike!

I like to use the basic stitches to create fun textures and patterns that are great for beginners and beyond. I have also added a range of new stitches and new techniques that are great for adding to your crochet skill list.

I love to design baby items, and over the years I have heard the question over and over: "Where are the patterns for baby boys?" Finding cute items for girls is easy, but I wanted to make sure we leveled the playing field. We have twin boys, and the task of finding cute boys patterns is fully understood! So in this book I have included designs for both boys and girls. Clothing, accessories, and more can be made for both, and I promise they will be a hit!

Do you like to make clothing? What about animals? Socks? Loafers? Blankets? This book is stuffed with so many cute patterns that you'll want to sink your hooks into!

Little Slugger Blanket

Wrap your little slugger in this squishy blanket! Fun colors and a playful one-row repeat stitch make this blanket fun to make and perfect for any baby.

Yarn

Red Heart Soft; medium weight #4; 100% acrylic; 5 oz (141 g) /256 yds (234 m) per skein

- 1 skein each: 4422 Tangerine (A), 9518 Teal (D), and 4600 White (E)
- 2 skeins each: 4604 Navy (B) and 9440 Light Gray Heather (C)

Hooks and Other Materials

- US size J-10 (6 mm) and I-9 (5.5 mm) crochet hooks
- Yarn needle

Finished Measurements

28 in. (71 cm) wide x 48 in. (122 cm) long

Gauge

14 sts x 16 rows = 4 in. (10 cm) in sc

Special Stitch

Long Single Crochet (long sc). Insert hook into specified stitch, pull up loop even with row, yarn over, and pull through loops on hook.

Pattern Note

- When changing colors, working the stitch before the color change, complete the stitch until the last pull through; drop working yarn, pull through next color as last pull through to complete color change, and finish stitch.

INSTRUCTIONS

With A, ch 94.

Row 1: 3 dc in 6th ch from hook, *ch 1, sk 3 chs, 3 dc in next ch, rep from * across, ending last rep with 2 dc (instead of 3) in last ch, changing to Color B in last st (see Pattern Note); turn.

Row 2: Ch 2, *dc in next ch-1 sp, tr in middle skipped ch in row 1, dc in same ch-1 sp, ch 1, rep from * across, ending last rep with 2 dc in top of beg skipped chs, changing to Color C in last st; turn.

Row 3: Ch 2, *dc in next ch-1 sp, tr in skipped st in row below, dc in same ch-1 sp, ch 1, rep from * across, ending last rep with 2 dc in top of turning ch, changing to next color in last st, changing to Color D (or next color in pattern); turn.

Rows 4–85: Rep row 3 for pattern, working in alternating rows of color A, B, C, D, E, ending on D. Join B to create border.

Border

Rnd 1: Turn, ch 1, 3 sc in first st, *sc in each st with long sc over ch into tr on Row 84, rep from * to last st of Row 85, 3 sc in last st, sc evenly across ends of rows, 3 sc in the first st of row 1, sc to last st, 3 sc in last st of row 1, sc even across ends of rows to Row 85, sl st to first st to join.

Rnds 2–8: Ch 1, sc in each st working 3 sc in second st of each 3 sc corner, join with sl st to first sc. Fasten off.

Cozy Panda Hat

Turn a basic hat pattern into the perfect accessory that is fun for dress up or cozy for every day. Just add ears and cute facial features for the most adorable panda!

Sizes
3–6 months, 9–12 months

Yarn
Knit Picks Mighty Stitch; medium weight #4; 80% acrylic, 20% superwash wool; 3.5 oz. (100 g)/208 yd. (190 m) per skein
- 1 skein each: 26807 White (A) and 26852 Black (B)

Hook and Other Materials
- US size G-6 (4 mm) crochet hook
- Yarn needle

Finished Measurements
3–6 months
Circumference: 14–16 in. (36–41 cm)
Hat height: 5.5 in. (14 cm)
9–12 months
Circumference: 16–18 in. (41–46 cm)
Hat height: 6 in. (15 cm)

Gauge
16 sts x 16 rows = 4 in. (10 cm) in sc

Special Stitches
Single Crochet 2 Together (sc2tog). (Insert hook, yarn over, pull up loop) in each of the stitches indicated, yarn over, draw through all loops on hook.
Double Crochet 2 Together (dc2tog). Yarn over, pull up a loop in next stitch, yarn over, pull through first 2 loops, yarn over, pull up a loop in the next stitch, yarn over and draw through first 2 loops, yarn over and pull through all loops on hook (counts as 1 dc).

Pattern Note
- The beginning ch-2 will not be counted as a stitch.

INSTRUCTIONS

3–6 months

With White, ch 4.

Rnd 1: 11 dc in first ch, join with sl st to first dc. (11 sts)

Rnd 2: Ch 2, 2 hdc in each st, join with sl st to first hdc. (22 sts)

Rnd 3: Ch 2, dc in the joining st, 2 dc in next st, *dc in next st, 2 dc in next st, rep from * around, join with sl st to first dc. (33 sts)

Rnd 4: Ch 2, hdc in the joining st, hdc in next st, 2 hdc in next st, *hdc in next 2 sts, 2 hdc in next st, rep from * around, join with sl st to first hdc. (44 sts)

Rnd 5: Ch 2, dc in the joining st, dc in next 2 sts, *dc in next 3 sts, 2 dc in next st, rep from * around, join with sl st first dc. (55 sts)

Rnd 6: Ch 2, hdc in the joining st, hdc in next 3 sts, *hdc in next 4 sts, 2 hdc in next st, rep from * around, join with sl st to first hdc. (66 sts)

Rnd 7: Ch 2, dc in each st around, join with sl st to first dc.

Rnd 8: Ch 2, hdc in each st around, join with sl st to first hdc.

Rnds 9–15: Rep rnds 7 and 8, ending on Rnd 7. Fasten off.

Rnd 16: Join Black, ch 1, sc in each st around, join with sl st to first sc.

Rnd 17: Ch 1, sc in next 15 sts, hdc in next st, (2 dc, ch 1, 2 dc) in next st, hdc in next st, sc in next 31 sts, hdc in next st, (2 dc, ch 1, 2 dc) in next st, hdc in next st, sc in next 14 sts, join with sl st to first sc to join.

Rnd 18: Ch 1, sc in next 12 sts, sc2tog (see Special Stitches), hdc in next 3 sts, (2dc, ch 1, 2 dc) in ch-1 sp, hdc in next 3 sts, sc2tog, sc in next 26 sts, sc2tog, hdc in next 3 sts, (2 dc, ch 1, 2 dc) in ch-1 sp, hdc in next 3 sts, sc2tog, sc in next 12 sts, join with sl st to first sc to join.

Rnd 19: Ch 2, hdc in next 10 sts, dc2tog (see Special Stitches), dc in next 6 sts, (2 dc, ch 1, 2 dc) in ch-1 sp, dc in next 6 sts, dc2tog, hdc in next 22 sts, dc2tog, dc in next 6 sts, (2 dc, ch 1, 2 dc) in ch-1 sp, dc in next 6 sts, dc2tog, hdc in next 10 sts, join with sl st to first hdc to join. Fasten off.

9–12 months

With White, Ch 4.

Rnd 1: 12 dc in first ch, join with sl st to first dc. (12 sts)

Rnd 2: Ch 2, 2 hdc in each st, join with sl st to first hdc. (24 sts)

Rnd 3: Ch 2, dc in joining st, 2 dc in next st, *dc in next st, 2 dc in next st, rep from * around, join with sl st to first dc. (36 sts)

Rnd 4: Ch 2, hdc in joining st, hdc in next st, *hdc in next 2 sts, 2 hdc in next st, rep from * around, join with sl st to first hdc. (48 sts)

Rnd 5: Ch 2, dc in joining st, dc in next 2 sts, *dc in next 3 sts, 2 dc in next st, rep from * around, join with sl st first dc. (60 sts)

Rnd 6: Ch 2, hdc in joining st, hdc in next 3 sts, *hdc in next 4 sts, 2 hdc in next st, rep from * around, join with sl st to first hdc. (72 sts)

Rnd 7: Ch 2, dc in each st around, join with sl st to first dc.

Rnd 8: Ch 2, hdc in each st around, join with sl st to first hdc.

Rnds 9–17: Rep rnds 7 and 8, ending on Rnd 7. Fasten off.

Rnd 18: Join Black, ch 1, sc in each st around, join with sl st to first sc.

Rnd 19: Ch 1, sc in next 17 sts, hdc in next st, (2 dc, ch 1, 2 dc) in next st, hdc in next st, sc in next 34 sts, hdc in next st, (2 dc, ch 1, 2 dc) in next st, hdc in next st, sc in next 16 sts, join with sl st to first sc to join.

Rnd 20: Ch 1, sc in next 14 sts, sc2tog (see Special Stitches), hdc in next 3 sts, (2dc, ch 1, 2 dc) in ch-1 sp, hdc in next 3 sts, sc2tog, sc in next 30 sts, sc2tog, hdc in next 3 sts, (2 dc, ch 1, 2 dc) in ch-1 sp, hdc in next 3 sts, sc2tog, sc in next 14 sts, join with sl st to first sc to join.

Rnd 21: Ch 2, hdc in next 12 sts, dc2tog (see Special Stitches), dc in next 6 sts, (2 dc, ch 1, 2 dc) in ch-1 sp, dc in next 6 sts, dc2tog, hdc in next 26 sts, dc2tog, dc in next 6 sts, (2 dc, ch 1, 2 dc) in ch-1 sp, dc in next 6 sts, dc2tog, hdc in next 12 sts, join with sl st to first hdc to join. Fasten off.

Both Sizes

Eyes

Black Patches

Rnd 1: With Black, ch 9, sc in second ch from hook, sc in next 3 chs, hdc in next 3 chs, hdc 4 in last ch, working in free loops of beginning ch, hdc in next 3 chs, sc in next 3 chs, 3 sc in last ch, join with sl st to first sc. (20 sts)

Rnd 2: Ch 1, sc in the same stitch as joining, sc in next st, hdc in next 3 sts, dc in next 2 sts, 2 dc in next 4 sts, dc in next 2 sts, hdc in next 3 sts, sc in next st, 2 sc in next 3 sts, join with sl st to first sc. (27 sts)

Rnd 3: Ch 1, hdc in the same st as joining, hdc in next 6 sts, (hdc in next st, 2 hdc in next st) 4

times, hdc in next 6 sts, (hdc in next st, 2 hdc in next st) 3 times, join with sl st to first hdc. (34 sts) Fasten off.

Nose
With Black, ch 3.

Row 1: Sc in the second ch from hook and in the next ch, turn. (2 sts)

Row 2: Ch 1, 2 sc in each st, turn. (4 sts)

Row 3: Ch 1, 2 sc in first st, sc in next 2 sts, 2 sc in last st, turn. (6 sts)

Row 4: Ch 1, sc in each st across, turn.

Row 5: Ch 1, sc evenly across the ends of rows, sc across bottom, sc evenly across the ends of rows on last edge, do not work across Row 5, join with sl st to first sc of Row 5. Fasten off, leaving long end for sewing.

Ears (make 2)
With Black, ch 2.

Rnd 1: 4 sc in second ch from hook, do not join. (4 sts)

Rnd 2: Working in the round throughout, 2 sc in each st. (8 sts)

Rnd 3: (Sc in next st, 2 sc in next st) around. (12 sts)

Rnds 4–6: Sc in each st around.

Rnd 7: (Sc in next st, sc2tog) around, join with a sl st to first st of rnd. Fasten off, leaving long end for sewing.

Assembly
Using photo as a guide, use yarn needle to sew the eyes, ears, and nose onto the hat.

Stitch an *X* in white on upper eye to finish.

Twinkles Tunic

What little darling doesn't need a simple, yet stunning, tunic? Mix and match with any leggings or a pair of ruffled pants for the perfect ensemble.

Size
9–12 months

Yarn
Lion Brand Vanna's Choice; light weight #3; 100% acrylic; 3.5 oz. (100 g)/254 yd. (232 m) per skein
- 2 skeins: 867-147 Purple
- 1 skein: 867-159 Mustard

Hook and Other Materials
- US size 7 (4.5 mm) crochet hook
- Yarn needle
- 1 stitch marker
- 2 buttons (1 in./2.5 cm)
- Sewing needle and matching thread

Finished Measurements
10 in. (25.4 cm) wide at chest x 12½ in. (31.75 cm) long

Gauge
15 sts x 6 rows = 4 in. (10 cm) in dc

Special Stitches
V-Stitch (V-st). (Dc, ch 2, dc) in stitch indicated.

Cluster (cl). Holding back last loop of each stitch on hook, 3 dc in stitch indicated, yarn over, pull through all loops on hook.

Shell. (Cl, ch 2, cl) in stitch indicated.

Single Crochet 2 Together (sc2tog). (Insert hook, yarn over, pull up loop) in each of the stitches indicated, yarn over, draw through all loops on hook.

Pattern Notes
- The Body panel is made first, followed by the Chest section. To finish, the straps are added and attached in the back with buttons.
- The beginning ch-4 counts as first dc plus ch 1.

INSTRUCTIONS

With Purple, ch 83.

Row 1 (RS): Dc in 5th ch from hook (first 4 chs count as first dc and ch-1), ch 2, sc in next ch, ch 3, sk next ch, sc in next ch, [ch 2, sk next 2 chs, V-st (see Special Stitches) in next ch, ch 2, sk next 2 chs, sc in next ch, ch 3, sk next ch, sc in next ch] across to last 3 chs, sk next 2 chs, (dc, ch 1, dc) in last st, turn.

Row 2: Ch 1, sc in first st, * ch 2, shell (see Special Stitches) in next ch-3 sp, ch 2 **, sc in ch sp of next V-st, rep from * across, ending last rep at **, sc in last st, turn.

Row 3: Ch 1, sc in first st, ch 1, sc in next ch-2 sp, * ch 2, V-st in ch-2 sp of next shell, ch 2, sc in next ch-2 sp **, ch 3, sc in next ch-2 sp, rep from * across, ending last rep at **, ch 1, sc in last st, turn.

Row 4: Ch 4 (see Pattern Notes), cl (see Special Stitches) in next ch-1 sp, * ch 2, sc in ch sp of next V-st, ch 2 **, shell in next ch-3 sp, rep from * across, ending last rep at **, cl in last ch-1 sp, ch 1, dc in last st, turn.

Row 5: Ch 4, dc in same st as beg ch-4, * ch 2, sc in next ch-2 sp, ch 3, sc in next ch-2 sp **, ch 2, V-st in ch sp of next shell, rep from * across, ending last rep at **, ch 2, (dc, ch 1, dc) in last st, turn.

Rows 6–20: Rep Rows 2–5, ending on Row 4.

Body Trim

Rnd 1: Working right into the Body Trim, ch 1, 3 sc in the first st, sc to the last st, 3 sc in the last st, sc evenly across ends of rows, 3 sc in first st of Row 1, sc to the last st, 3 sc in the last st, sc evenly across ends of rows, join with sl st to the first sc. Fasten off.

Top Trim

Rnd 1: Overlap the first and last 5 sts of Row 20 and Body Trim. Working through both stitches, join Purple, ch 1, sc 5 through both stitches, sc in each st around, join with sl st to first sc. (87 sts)

Rnd 2: Ch 1, * sc in next 8 sts, sc2tog (see Special Stitches), rep from * around, join with sl st to first sc. (77 sts)

Rnd 3: (*Note:* Mark the 25th st of Rnd.) Ch 1, sc in each st around, join with sl st to first sc. Fasten off.

Chest

Row 1: Join in marked 25th st in Top Trim, ch 1, sc in next 31 sts, turn. (31 sts)

Row 2: Sc2tog twice, sc in next 23 sts, sc2tog twice, turn. (27 sts)

Row 3: Sc2tog, sc in next 23 sts, sc2tog, turn. (25 sts)

Rows 4–12: Ch 1, sc in each st across, turn.

Row 13: Sc2tog, sc in next 21 sts, sc2tog, turn. (23 sts)

Row 14: Sc2tog, sc in next 19 sts, sc2tog, turn. (21 sts)

Trim

Row 15: Ch 1, 3 sc in first st, sc in next 19 sts, 3 sc in last st, sc evenly across ends of rows, sc around back, sc evenly across ends of rows up side of Chest, join with sl st to first sc. Fasten off.

Straps

Right

Row 1: Join in the first st on Right side of Chest, ch 1, sc in next 4 sts, turn.

Rows 2–35: Ch 1, sc in each st across, turn.

Row 36: Ch 1, sc in first st, ch 2, sk 2 sts, sc in last st, turn.

Row 37: Ch 1, sc in first st, 2 sc in ch-2 sp, sc in last st, turn.

Row 38: Sc2tog twice. Fasten off.

Left

Row 1: Join in the fourth st from the left edge, ch 1, sc in next 4 sts, turn.

Rows 2–35: Ch 1, sc in each st across, turn.

Row 36: Ch 1, sc in first st, ch 2, sk 2 sts, sc in last st, turn.

Row 37: Ch 1, sc in first st, 2 sc in ch-2 sp, sc in last st, turn.

Row 38: Sc2tog twice. Fasten off.

Bow (make 2)

With Mustard, ch 5.

Row 1: 5 tr in first ch, ch 4, sl st to first center ch, ch 4, 5 tr in first center ch, ch 4, sl st to center ch. Fasten off.

Wrap center of bow 10 times.

Finishing

Sew buttons on the back 6–8 stitches from the middle. Crisscross the straps and slip over button.

Use yarn needle to attach bows to front at joining of the strap on the Chest.

Baby's First Dino

Spikes, dangly legs, and a plump body make up this adorable dino. It's perfect for any level of crocheter to try their first amigurumi . . . and for baby's first dino!

Yarn

Plymouth Yarn Encore Worsted; medium weight #4; 75% acrylic, 25% wool; 3.5 oz. (100 g)/200 yd. (183 m) per skein
- 1 skein each: 215 Yellow (A) and 1317 Vacation Blues (B)

Hook and Other Materials
- US size F-5 (3.75 mm) crochet hook
- Yarn needle
- Stitch markers
- Poly-fil stuffing

Finished Measurements
6½ in. (16.5 cm) long

Gauge
8 sts x 9 rows = 2 in. (5 cm) in sc

Special Stitch
Single Crochet 2 Together (sc2tog). (Insert hook, yarn over, pull up loop) in each of the sts indicated, yarn over, draw through all loops on hook.

Pattern Notes
- The pattern will begin at the tail and finish at the head.
- The spikes, legs, and face will be added to finish.
- Place marker in first stitch of round to indicate beginning of round.

INSTRUCTIONS

With Color A, ch 2.

Rnd 1: 3 sc in second ch from hook; do not join. (3 sts)

Rnd 2: Working in the round, 2 sc in each st. (6 sts)

Rnd 3: Sc in each st around.

Rnd 4: (Sc in next st, 2 sc in next st) around. (9 sts)

Rnd 5: (Sc in next 2 sts, 2 sc in next st) around. (12 sts)

Rnd 6: Sc in each st around.

Rnd 7: 2 sc in next 7 sts, sc in next 5 sts. (19 sts)

Rnd 8: (Sc in next st, 2 sc in next st) 7 times, sc in next 5 sts. (26 sts)

Rnd 9: Sc in each st around.

Rnd 10: (Sc in next 3 sts, 2 sc in next st) 4 times, sc in next 10 sts. (30 sts)

Rnds 11–16: Sc in each st around.

Rnd 17: (Sc in next 4 sts, 2 sc in next st) 4 times, sc in next 10 sts. (34 sts)

Rnd 18: Sc in each st around.

Rnd 19: (Sc in next 4 sts, sc2tog; see Special Stitch) 4 times, sc in next 10 sts. (30 sts)

Rnd 20: (Sc in next 3 sts, sc2tog) 4 times, sc in next 10 sts. (26 sts)

Rnd 21: Sc in each st around.

Rnd 22: (Sc in next 2 sts, sc2tog) 5 times, sc in next 6 sts. (21 sts)

Rnd 23: (Sc in next st, sc2tog) 5 times, sc in next 6 sts. (16 sts)

Rnd 24: Sc in each st around.

Rnd 25: Sc in next st, 2 sc in next 8 sts, sc in next 7 sts. (24 sts)

Rnd 26: Sc in next st, (sc in next st, 2 sc in next st) 8 times, sc in next 7 sts. (32 sts)

Rnds 27–29: Sc in each st around.

Rnd 30: Sc in next st, (sc in next st, sc2tog) 8 times, sc in next 7 sts. (24 sts)

Rnd 31: Sc in next st, sc2tog 8 times, sc in next 7 sts. (16 sts) Stuff body with Poly-fil stuffing.

Rnd 32: Sc2tog 8 times. (8 sts)

Rnd 33: Sc in next 8 sts, sl st to the first st to join. Fasten off.

Use yarn needle to sew Rnd 33 closed.

Spikes

Working from tip of tail to base of neck, crochet in a straight line within the stitches in the body, using them as your stitches.

Row 1: Join Color B, * (Ch 3, tr in same st), dc in next st, hdc in next st, sc in next st, sl st to next st, rep from * to base of neck. Fasten off.

Legs (make 4)

With Color B, ch 2.

Rnd 1: 5 sc in second ch from hook, join with sl st to first sc. Fasten off. (5 sts)

Rnd 2: Join Color A, ch 1, 2 sc in each st around, join with sl st to first sc. (10 sts)

Rnd 3: Ch 1, sc in each st around, do not join.

Rnds 4–9: Working in the round, sc in each st around. Stuff legs loosely with Poly-fil stuffing. Fasten off, leaving long end for sewing.

Finishing

Use yarn needle to stitch each leg onto body. Stitch on eyes with yarn needle and Color B.

Itty-Bitty Britches

Crochet a cute pair of these itty-bitty britches for the new "itty-bitty" in your family. Made in a bulky weight yarn, these work up fast and easy.

Size
Newborn

Yarn
Knit Picks Billow; bulky weight #5; 100% cotton; 3.5 oz. (100 g)/120 yd. (110 m) per skein
- 1 skein each: 26231 Gosling (A), 26222 Natural (B)

Hooks and Other Materials
- US size J-10 (6 mm) and H-8 (5 mm) crochet hooks
- Yarn needle

Finished Measurements
7½ in. (19 cm) wide x 11 in. (28 cm) long

Gauge
With J (6 mm) crochet hook:
6 sts x 5 rows = 2 in. (5 cm) in hdc

Special Stitches
Front Post Double Crochet (FPdc). Yarn over, insert hook from front to back around post of st indicated, yarn over and pull up a loop (3 loops on hook), (yarn over and draw through 2 loops on hook) twice.

Back Post Single Crochet (BPsc). Insert hook from back to front around post of st indicated, yarn over and pull up a loop, yarn over and draw through 2 loops on hook.

Pattern Notes
- The pants are made from the waist down. The knee tabs will be made separately and sewn on to finish.
- The beginning ch-2 will not count as a stitch unless otherwise indicated.

INSTRUCTIONS

With J-10 (6 mm) hook and Color A, ch 43.

Rnd 1(WS): Sc in second ch from hook and in each ch around, join with sl st to first sc. (42 sts)

Rnd 2: Ch 2, FPdc (see Special Stitches) in each st, join with sl st to first FPdc.

Rnds 3–4: Ch 2, FPdc on each FPdc around, join with sl st to first FPdc. Fasten off.

Rnd 5 (RS): Turn, join Color B in first st, ch 2, hdc in each st around, join with sl st to first hdc.

Rnds 6–12: Ch 2, hdc in each st around, join with sl st to first hdc.

Leg 1

Rnd 13: Ch 2, hdc 21, leave remaining sts unworked, join with sl st to first hdc. (21 sts)

Rnd 14: Ch 1, sc in first st, hdc in next 20 sts, do not join.

Rnds 15–22: Working in the rnd, hdc in each st around. Fasten off.

Rnd 23: Join Color A in first st, ch 1, sc in each st around, join with sl st to first sc.

Rnds 24–25: Ch 1, BPsc (see Special Stitches) in each st around, join with sl st to first BPsc. Fasten off.

Leg 2

Rnd 13: Join in next unworked st, ch 1, hdc in each st around, join with sl st to first hdc. (21 sts)

Rnd 14: Ch 1, sc in first st, hdc in next 20 sts; do not join.

Rnds 15–22: Working in the rnd, hdc in each st around. Fasten off.

Rnd 23: Join Color A in first st, ch 1, sc in each st around, join with sl st to first sc.

Rnds 24–25: Ch 1, BPsc (see Special Stitches) in each st around, join with sl st to first BPsc. Fasten off.

Knee Tab (make 2)

With H (5 mm) hook and Color A, ch 5.

Rnd 1: Sc in second ch from hook, sc in next 2 chs, 3 sc in last ch, working in free loops of beginning ch, sc in next 2 chs, 3 sc in last ch, join with sl st to first sc. (10 sts)

Rnd 2: Ch 1, sc in joining st, sc in next 2 sts, 2 sc in next 3 sts, sc in next 2 sts, 2 sc in next 3 sts, join with sl st to first sc. Fasten off, leaving long end for sewing. (16 sts)

Finishing

Use yarn needle to sew Knee Tab onto each Leg.

Sweetums Circle Vest

This circle vest is made in a quick 13-round pattern. You'll have one made for your little girl before you know it! It is perfect for any season and wardrobe.

Size
9–12 months

Yarn
Premier Yarns Everyday Collection; medium weight #4; 100% acrylic; 4 oz. (113 g)/203 yd. (186 m) per skein
- 1 skein: E0100-51 Spa

Hook and Other Materials
- US size I-9 (5.5 mm) crochet hook
- Yarn needle
- Stitch markers

Finished Measurements
17 in. (43 cm) wide

Gauge
8 sts x 4 rows = 2 in. (5 cm) in dc

Special Stitches
Picot. Ch 3, sl st to the first ch.

Double Crochet 2 Together (dc2tog). Yarn over, pull up a loop in next st, yarn over, pull through first 2 loops, yarn over, pull up a loop in the next stitch, yarn over and draw through first 2 loops, yarn over, pull through all loops on hook (counts as 1 dc).

Double Crochet 3 Together (dc3tog). Yarn over, pull up a loop in next st, yarn over, pull through first 2 loops, (yarn over pull up a loop in the next st, yarn over and draw through first 2 loops) twice, yarn over, pull through all loops on hook (counts as 1 dc).

Double Crochet 4 Together (dc4tog). Yarn over, pull up a loop in next st, yarn over, pull through first 2 loops, (yarn over pull up a loop in the next st, yarn over and draw through first 2 loops) three times, yarn over, pull through all loops on hook (counts as 1 dc).

Pattern Notes

- The vest is made from the center out.
- The beginning ch-4 counts as first dc plus ch 1.
- The beginning ch-6 counts as first dc plus ch 3.
- The beginning ch-3 counts as first dc.
- The beginning ch-2 of a round will not count as a stitch unless otherwise indicated.

INSTRUCTIONS

Rnd 1: Ch 4 (see Pattern Notes), picot (see Special Stitches), ch 1, (dc, ch 1) 7 times in first ch, join with sl st to ch-3 of beg ch-4.

Rnd 2: Ch 4, picot, ch 2, dc in ch-1 sp, ch-1, picot, ch 2, * dc in ch-1 sp, ch 1, picot, ch 2, rep from *, join with sl st in ch-3 of beg ch-4.

Rnd 3: Ch 4, picot, ch 1, dc in ch-2 sp, ch 1, picot, ch 1, dc in next dc,* ch 1, picot, ch 1, dc in ch-2, ch 1, picot, ch 1 ** , dc in next dc, rep from *, ending at last rep at **, join with sl st to ch-3 of beg ch-4.

Rnd 4: Ch 6 (see Pattern Notes), * dc in dc, ch 3, rep from * around, join with sl st to ch-3 of beg ch-6.

Rnd 5: Ch 3 (see Pattern Notes), * 3 dc in ch-3 sp, dc in dc, (dc, ch 1, 2 dc) in ch-3 sp, 2 dc in dc, (2 dc, ch 1, dc) in ch-3 sp, dc in next dc, 3 dc in ch-3 sp **, (dc, ch 1, dc) in dc, rep from * around, ending last rep at **, join with sl st in ch-3 of beg ch-3.

Rnd 6: Ch 3, dc in next 5 dc, ch 2, sk ch-1 sp, * dc in next 6 dc, ch 2, sk ch-1 sp, rep from * around, join with sl st in ch-3 of beg ch-3.

Rnd 7: Ch 2 (see Pattern Notes), dc in next 3 dc, dc2tog (see Special Stitches), (ch 2, dc in ch-2 sp, ch 2), * dc2tog, dc in next 2 sts, dc2tog, (ch 2, dc in ch-2 sp, ch 2), rep from * around, join with sl st in first dc.

Rnd 8: (*Note:* Armholes will be created in this round.) Ch 2, dc3tog (see Special Stitches), ch 4, 2 dc in dc, ch 4, dc4tog (see Special Stitches), ch 4, 2 dc in dc, ch 4, * dc in next dc, ch 2, sk 11 sts, dc in next dc, ch 4, 2 dc in next dc, ch 4 **, [dc4tog, ch 4, 2 dc in next dc, ch 4] 6 times, rep from * around, ending last rep at **, join with sl st to top of beg dc3tog.

Rnd 9: Ch 3, 4 dc in ch-4 sp, dc in next 2 dc, 4 dc in ch-4 sp, dc in top of dc4tog, 4 dc in ch-4 sp, dc in next 2 dc, 4 dc in ch-4 sp, dc in next dc, 14 dc in ch-12 sp, dc in next dc, [4 dc in next ch-4 sp, dc in next 2 dc, 4 dc in next ch-4 sp, dc in top of dc4tog] 6 times, 4 dc in next ch-4 sp, dc in next 2 dc, dc in next ch-4 sp, dc in next dc, 14 dc in ch-12 sp, dc in next dc, 4 dc in ch-4 sp, dc in next 2 dc, 4 dc in ch-4 sp, join with sl st to ch-3 of beg ch-3.

Rnd 10: Ch 2, dc2tog, sk 1 st, ch 4, * dc3tog, sk 1 st, ch 4, rep from * around to last 3 sts, dc3tog, ch 4, join with sl st to top of dc2tog. (144 sts)

Rnd 11: Ch 3, dc in same st, * (3 dc in ch-3 sp, dc in next dc) 3 times, 3 dc in ch-3 sp **, 2 dc in next dc, rep from * around, ending last rep at **, join with sl st in ch-3 of beg ch-3.

Rnd 12: Ch 1, sc, * ch 5, sk 3 sts, sc in next st, rep from * around to last 5 sts, ch 2, join with tr in first sc.

Rnd 13: Ch 1, sc, * ch 5, sc in next ch-5 sp, rep from * until 1 ch-sp remains, ch 2, join with tr in first sc. Fasten off.

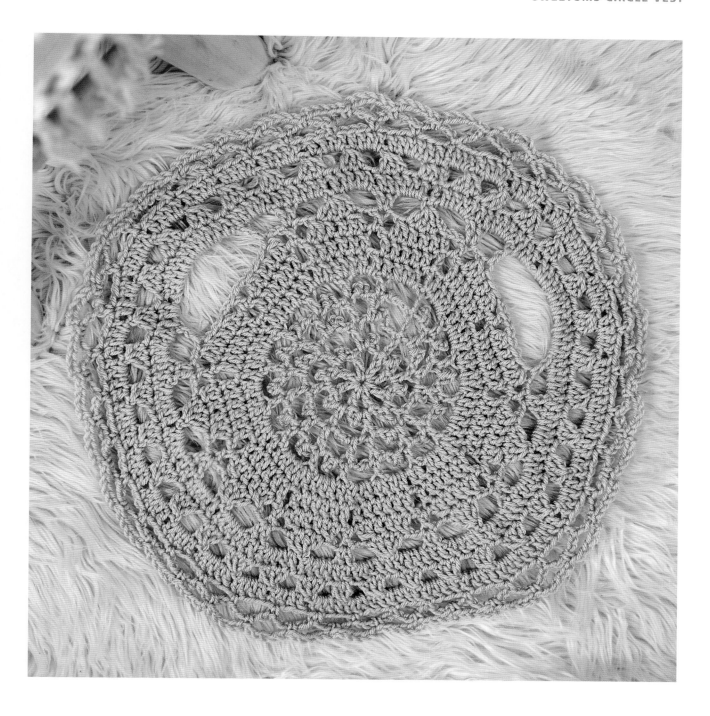

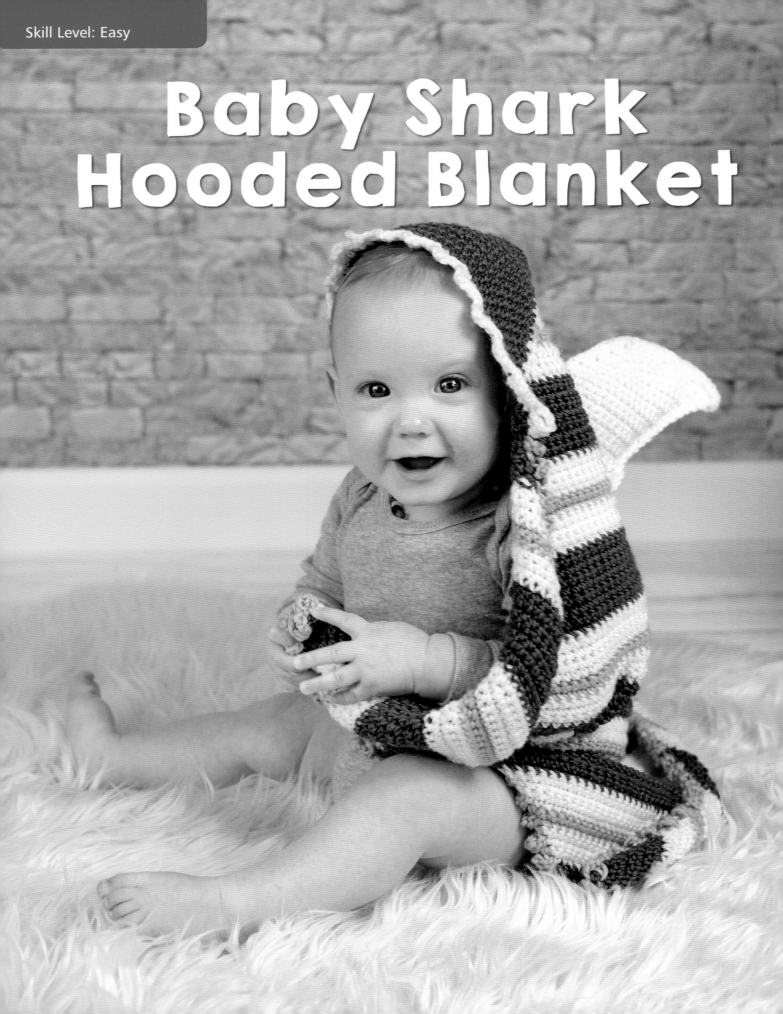

Baby Shark
Hooded Blanket

*Your sweet one will love to cuddle in this delightful hooded shark blanket!
It is also a good spark for baby's imagination.*

Yarn

Red Heart Chic Sheep; medium
   weight #4; 100% merino
   wool; 3.5 oz. (100 g)/186
   yd. (170 m) per skein
• 3 skeins: 5640 Platinum
• 2 skeins each: 5311 Lace,
   5675 Creme de Mint, 5641
   Sterling

Hook and Other Materials

• US size J-10 (6 mm) crochet
   hook
• Yarn needle
• Poly-fil stuffing

Finished Measurements

Blanket: 32 in. (81 cm) wide x
   27 in. (69 cm) long

Gauge

16 sts x 18 rows = 4 in.
   (10 cm) in sc

Special Stitches

**Single Crochet 2 Together
   (sc2tog).** (Insert hook, yarn
   over, pull up loop) in each
   of the sts indicated, yarn over, draw through all loops on hook.
Back Post Slip Stitch (BP sl st). Insert hook from back to front around around post
   of st indicated, pull up a loop and draw through loop on hook.
Front Post Slip Stitch (FP sl st). Insert hook from front to back around post
   of st indicated, pull up a loop and draw through loop on hook.

Pattern Note

• When changing colors, complete the stitch until the last pull through; drop working
   yarn, pull through next color as last pull through to complete color change and
   finish stitch.

Color Sequence
Rows 1–6: Platinum
Rows 7–10: Lace (4 rows)
Rows 11–12: Creme de Mint (2 rows)
Rows 13–16: Lace (4 rows)
Rows 17–24: Platinum (8 rows)
Repeat Color Rows 7–24 until you complete
    Row 116.

INSTRUCTIONS
With Platinum, ch 2.
Row 1: 2 sc in first chain, turn. (2 sts)
Row 2: Ch 1, 2 sc in each st, turn. (4 sts)
Row 3: Ch 1, 2 sc in first st, sc in next 2 sts, 2 sc in
    last st, turn. (6 sts)
Row 4: Ch 1, 2 sc in first st, sc in each st to last st,
    2 sc in last st, turn. Increase by 2 sts.
Repeat Row 4 until Row 60, also following Color
    Sequence. At the end of Row 60, you will have
    120 sts.
Rows 61–116: Ch 1, sc, sc2tog (see Special
    Stitches), sc until 3 sts remain, sc2tog, sc in last
    st, turn. (*Note:* Each row will decrease by 2 sts.)

Rows 117–143 (Hood): Using Platinum through-
    out, ch 1, 2 sc in first st, sc to next to last st, 2 sc
    in last st. (*Note:* Each row will increase by 2 sts.)
Fasten off, leaving a long end for sewing.

Teeth
Row 1: With Lace, sl st in first st on RS, * (sc, ch
    3, tr) in next st, dc in next st, hdc in next st, rep
    from * across edge of hood, sl st to last st. Fasten
    off.

Border
Rnd 1: Join Creme de Mint at edge of hood on sc
    post, ch 4, BP sl st (see Special Stitches), ch 4,
    FP sl st (see Special Stitches), ch 4, rep from *
    around to opposite side of hood, join with sl st
    to post. Fasten off.

Fin (make 2)
With Lace, ch 20.
Row 1: Sc in second ch from hook and in each
    across, turn. (19 sts)

Row 2: Sc2tog, sc 15, sc2tog, turn. (17 sts)

Row 3: Sc2tog, sc13, sc2tog, turn. (15 sts)

Row 4: Ch 1, sc in each st across, turn.

Row 5: Sc2tog, sc 11, sc2tog, turn. (13 sts)

Row 6: Ch 1, sc in each st across, turn.

Row 7: Sc2tog, sc 9, sc2tog, turn. (11 sts)

Row 8: Ch 1, sc in each st across, turn.

Row 9: Sc2tog, sc 7, sc2tog, turn. (9 sts)

Row 10: Ch 1, sc in each st across, turn.

Row 11: Sc2tog, sc 5, sc2tog, turn. (7 sts)

Row 12: Ch 1, sc in each st across, turn.

Row 13: Sc2tog, sc 3, sc2tog, turn. (5 sts)

Row 14: Ch 1, 2 sc in first st, sc to last 2 sts, sc2tog, turn.

Row 15: Sc2tog, sc to last st, 2 sc in last st, turn.

Rows 16–17: Rep Row 14 and Row 15.

Row 18: Ch 1, 2 sc in first st, sc to last 4 sts, sc2tog twice, turn.

Row 19: Sc2tog, leave remaining 3 sts unworked. Fasten off.

Finishing

Use yarn needle and sew fin panels together, leaving bottom unworked.

Stuff with Poly-fil and sew bottom of fin to back of blanket.

Blossom Bib

Keep your baby squeaky clean with this classic mandala-style bib. Make one in every color!

Yarn

Knit Picks Shine Worsted; medium weight #4; 60% pima cotton, 40% modal; 1.8 oz. (50 g)/75 yd. (69 m) per skein
- 1 skein: 6563 Cream

Hook and Other Materials
- US size F-5 (3.75 mm) crochet hook
- Yarn needle

Finished Measurements

7 in. (18 cm) wide

Gauge

5 sts x 2 rows = 1 in. (2.5 cm) in dc

Pattern Notes
- The beginning ch-3 counts as the first dc.
- The beginning ch-4 counts as the first dc plus ch 1.

INSTRUCTIONS

Ch 6, join in first ch to form ring.

Rnd 1: Ch 3 (see Pattern Notes), 19 dc in ring, join with sl st to beg ch-3.

Rnd 2: Ch 3, * dc in next st, ch 2, dc in next st, rep from * until first remains, dc in last st, ch 2, join with sl st to beg ch-3.

Rnd 3: Sl st in next st, sl st in ch-sp, (ch 3, dc, ch 2, 2 dc) in same ch-sp, (2 dc, ch 2, 2 dc) in each ch-sp around, join with sl st to beg ch-3.

Rnd 4: Sl st in next st, sl st in ch-sp, (ch 3, 2 dc, ch 2, 3 dc) in ch-sp, * sk 1 dc, sl st between next 2 dc sts **, (3 dc, ch 1, 3 dc) in next ch-sp, rep from * around, ending last rep at **, join with sl st to beg ch-3.

Rnd 5: Ch 4 (see Pattern Notes), dc in same st, * ch 2, sc in ch-1 sp, ch 2 **, (dc, ch 1, dc) in sl st, rep from * around, ending last rep at **, join with sl st to ch-3 of beg ch-4. (80 sts)

Rnd 6: Ch 3, dc in ch-1 sp, dc in next dc, 2 dc in ch-2 sp, 2 dc in sc, * 2 dc in ch-2 sp, dc in next dc, dc in ch-1 sp, dc in next dc, 2 dc in ch-2 sp, dc in sc, 2 dc in ch-2 sp**, dc in next dc, dc in ch-1 sp, dc in next dc, 2 dc in ch-2 sp, 2 dc in sc, rep from * ending last rep at **, join with sl st in beg ch-3. (85 sts)

Rnd 7: Ch 3, dc in each dc around, join with sl st to beg ch-3. Fasten off.

Rnd 8: (*Note:* This round includes ties.) Ch 45, sl st into any st, * sk 2 sts, 6 dc in next st, sk 2 sts, sl st in next st, rep from * 10 times, ch 46, sc in second ch from hook and in each ch across to last ch, sl st in same st as beg ch-46, sc in next 5 sts, sl st in next 8 sts, sc in next 5 sts, sl st in next st of beg ch 45, sc in each ch to end. Fasten off.

Sprinkle Socks

Keep those tiny toes toasty with these adorable socks. This pattern is great for beginners, as it uses only basic stitches and the sock is made from toe to cuff. I'm sure you'll love these baby socks and make multiple sets for every outfit!

Sizes
3–6 months, 9–12 months

Yarn
Knit Picks Hawthorne Fingering; fine weight #2; 80% superwash fine highland wool, 20% polyamide (nylon); 3.5 oz. (100 g)/357 yd. (326 m) per skein
- 1 skein: 27221 Italian Ice Speckle

Hook and Other Materials
- US size C-2 (2.75 mm) crochet hook
- Yarn needle

Finished Measurements
Toe to back of heel:
3–6 months: 3½ in. (9 cm)
9–12 months: 4 in. (10 cm)

Gauge
16 sts x 16 rows = 4 in. (10 cm) in sc

Special Stitches
Single Crochet 2 Together (sc2tog). Pull up a loop in each of next 2 sc, yarn over and draw through all 3 loops on hook (counts as 1 sc).
Front Post Double Crochet (FPdc). Yarn over, insert hook from front to back around post of st indicated, yarn over and pull up a loop (3 loops on hook), (yarn over and draw through 2 loops on hook) twice.
Back Post Double Crochet (BPdc). Yarn over, insert hook from back to front around post of st indicated, yarn over and pull up a loop (3 loops on hook), (yarn over and draw through 2 loops on hook) twice.

Pattern Notes
- The socks are crocheted from the toe to cuff.
- The beginning ch-3 counts as the first dc.
- The beginning ch-2 will not count as a stitch unless otherwise indicated.

INSTRUCTIONS

3–6 months

Toe/Foot

Ch 2.

Rnd 1: 8 sc in second ch from hook, do not join. (8 sts)

Rnd 2: Working in the round, 2 sc in each st. (16 sts)

Rnd 3: (Sc in next st, 2 sc in next st) around. (24 sts)

Rnd 4: (Sc in next 2 sts, 2 sc in next st) around. (32 sts)

Rnds 5–22: Sc in each st around.

Heel

Row 23: Sc in next 16 sts, leaving remaining sts unworked, turn. (16 sts)

Rows 24–28: Ch 1, sc in each st across, turn.

Row 29: Ch 1, sc in next 4 sts, sc2tog (see Special Stitches) 4 times, sc in next 4 sts, turn. (12 sts)

Row 30: Ch 1, sc in next 4 sts, sc2tog 2 times, sc in next 4 sts. (10 sts)

Ankle

Rnd 31: Sl st to the first st of rnd, ch 1, using ends of rows as sts, sc 8, sc 16 across Foot, using ends of rows as sts, sc 8, join with sl st to first sc. (32 sts)

Rnd 32: Ch 1, sc in each st around, join with sl st to first sc. (32 sts)

Cuff

Rnd 33: Ch 3, dc in next st, ch 2, sk 2, * dc in next 2 sts, ch 2, sk 2, rep from * around, join with sl st to beg ch-3.

Rnd 34: Ch 3, dc in each ch and st around, join with sl st to beg ch-3.

Rnd 35: Ch 1, sc in each st around, join with sl st to first sc.

Rnds 36–37: Ch 2, FPdc (see Special Stitches) on next st, BPdc (see Special Stitches) on next st, rep from * around, join with sl st to first FPdc. Fasten off.

Finishing

Sew heel closed with yarn needle.

9–12 months

Toe/Foot

Ch 2.

Rnd 1: 8 sc in second ch from hook, do not join. (8 sts)

Rnd 2: Working in the rnd, 2 sc in each st. (16 sts)

Rnd 3: (Sc in next st, 2 sc in next st) around. (24 sts)

Rnd 4: (Sc in next 2 sts, 2 sc in next st) around. (32 sts)

Rnd 5: (Sc in next 7 sts, 2 sc in next st) around. (36 sts)

Rnds 6–26: Sc in each st around.

Heel

Row 27: Sc in next 16 sts, leaving remaining sts unworked, turn. (16 sts)

Rows 28–32: Ch 1, sc in each st across, turn.

Row 33: Ch 1, sc in next 4 sts, sc2tog (see Special Stitches) 4 times, sc in next 4 sts, turn. (12 sts)

Row 34: Ch 1, sc in next 4 sts, sc2tog 2 times, sc in next 4 sts. (10 sts)

Ankle

Rnd 35: Sl st to the first st of rnd, ch 1, using ends of rows as sts, sc 8, sc 16 across Foot, using ends of rows as sts, sc 8, join with sl st to first sc. (32 sts)

Rnd 36: Ch 1, sc in each st around, join with sl st to first sc. (32 sts)

Cuff

Rnd 37: Ch 3, dc in next st, ch 2, sk 2, * dc in next 2 sts, ch 2, sk 2, rep from * around, join with sl st to beg ch-3.

Rnd 38: Ch 3, dc in each ch and st around, join with sl st to beg ch-3.

Rnd 39: Ch 1, sc in each st around, join with sl st to first sc.

Rnds 40–41: Ch 2, FPdc (see Special Stitches) on next st, BPdc (see Special Stitches) on next st, rep from * around, join with sl st to first FPdc. Fasten off.

Finishing

Sew heel closed with yarn needle.

Limelight
Newborn Hat

Keep your newborn's noggin and hands warm with this sweet and easy set (matching mittens begin on page 42).

Size
Newborn

Yarn
Cascade Yarns Cherub Aran; medium weight #4; 55% nylon, 45% acrylic; 3.5 oz. (100 g)/240 yd. (220 m) per skein
- 1 skein each: 09 Ecru, 56 Lime Chiffon, 17 Grey

Hook and Other Materials
- US size F-5 (3.75 mm) crochet hook
- Yarn needle

Finished Measurements
Circumference: 12–14 in. (30.5–35.6 cm)
Hat height: 5.5–6 in. (14–15.2 cm)

Gauge
5 sts x 3 rows = 1 in. (2.5 cm) in dc

Pattern Notes
- The beginning ch-2 will not count as a stitch.
- When changing colors, complete the stitch until the last pull through; drop working yarn, pull through next color as last pull through to complete color change and finish stitch.

INSTRUCTIONS

With Ecru, ch 4.

Rnd 1: 8 dc in first ch, join with sl st to first dc. (8 sts)

Rnd 2: Ch 2 (see Pattern Notes), 2 dc in each st, join with sl st to first dc. Join Lime, fasten off Ecru (see Pattern Notes). (16 sts)

Rnd 3: Ch 1, (sc in next st, 2 sc in next) around, join with sl st to first sc. Join Ecru, fasten off Lime. (24 sts)

Rnd 4: Ch 2, (dc in next 2 sts, 2 dc in next st) around, join with sl st to first dc. (32 sts)

Rnd 5: Ch 2, (dc in next 3 sts, 2 dc in next st) around, join with sl st to first dc. Join Lime, fasten off Ecru. (40 sts)

Rnd 6: Ch 1, (sc in next 4 sts, 2 dc in next st around), join with sl st to first sc. Join Ecru, fasten off Lime. (48 sts)

Rnds 7–8: Ch 2, dc in each st around, join with sl st to first dc. Join Lime, fasten off Ecru.

Rnd 9: Ch 1, sc in each st around, join with sl st to first sc. Join Ecru, fasten off Lime.

Rnds 10–11: Ch 2, dc in each st around, join with sl st to first dc. Join Lime, fasten off Ecru.

Rnd 12: Ch 1, sc in each st around, join with sl st to first sc. Join Grey, fasten off Lime.

Rnd 13: Ch 2, hdc in each st around, join with sl st to first hdc.

Rnds 14–16: Ch 2, hdc in each back horizontal bar of previous rnd hdc, join with sl st to first hdc. Fasten off.

Tab

With Lime, ch 13.

Row 1: Sc in second ch from hook and in each ch across, turn. (12 sts)

Rows 2–3: Ch 1, sc in each st across. Fasten off.

Finishing

Use yarn needle and Grey to sew tab over edge of beanie.

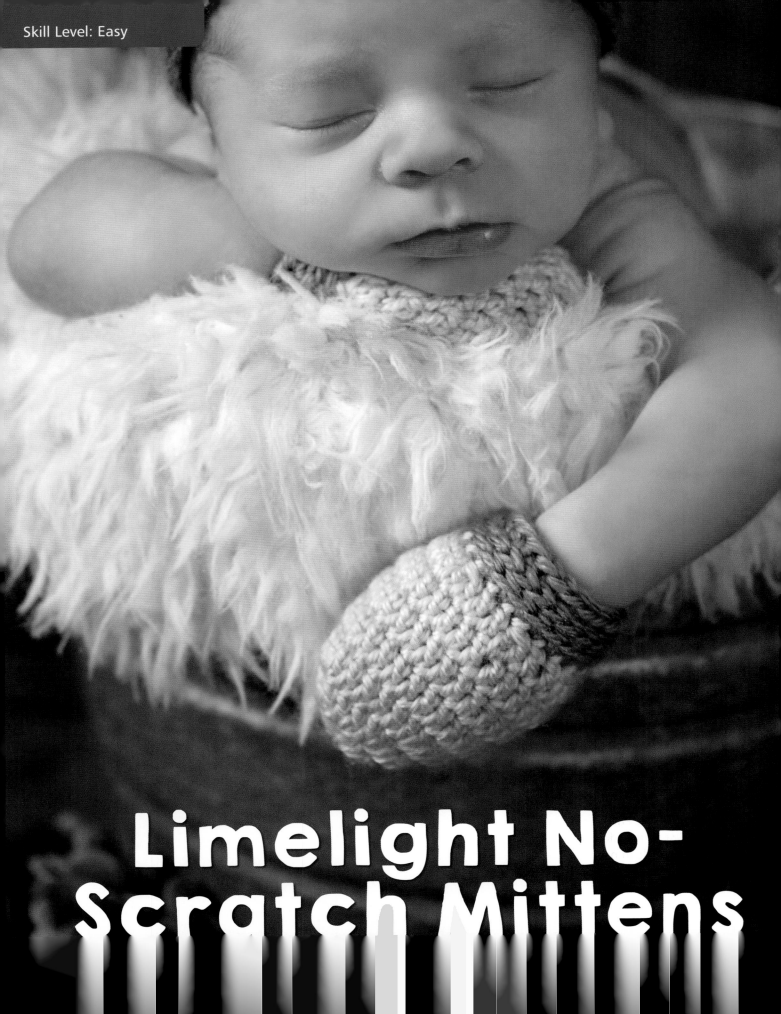

Limelight No-Scratch Mittens

These mittens will keep baby's hands warm, or use them as no-scratch mitts to protect the sweet baby's face.

Size
Newborn

Yarn
Cascade Yarns Cherub Aran; medium weight #4; 55% nylon, 45% acrylic; 3.5 oz. (100 g)/240 yd. (220 m) per skein
• 1 skein each: 56 Lime Chiffon, 17 Grey

Hook and Other Materials
• US size F-5 (3.75 mm) crochet hook
• Yarn needle

Finished Measurements
3 in. (7.5 cm) long

Gauge
5 sts x 3 rows = 1 in. (2.5 cm) in dc

Special Stitch
Double Crochet 2 Together (dc2tog). Yarn over, pull up a loop in next st, yarn over, pull through first 2 loops, yarn over, pull up a loop in the next stitch, yarn over and draw through first 2 loops, yarn over pull through all loops on hook (counts as 1 dc).

Pattern Notes
• The beginning ch-2 will not count as a stitch unless otherwise indicated.
• When changing colors, complete the stitch until the last pull through; drop working yarn, pull through next color as last pull through to complete color change and finish stitch.

INSTRUCTIONS
Make 2
With Lime, ch 4.
Rnd 1: 10 dc in first chain, join with sl st to first dc. (10 dc)
Rnd 2: Ch 2 (see Pattern Notes), 2 dc in each st, join with sl st to first dc. (20 dc)
Rnd 3: Ch 2, (dc in next 4 sts, 2 dc in next st) around, join with sl st to first dc. (24 sts)
Rnds 4–6: Ch 2, dc in each st around, join with sl st to first dc.

Rnd 7: Ch 2, (dc 2, dc2tog; see Special Stitch) 6 times, join with sl st to first dc. Join Gray, fasten off Lime (see Pattern Notes). (18 sts)
Rnd 8: Ch 2, hdc in each st around, join with sl st to first hdc.
Rnds 9–10: Ch 2, hdc in each back horizontal bar of previous rnd hdc, join with sl st to first hdc. Fasten off.

Under the Sea Mobile

Catch your baby's attention with this whimsical underwater-themed mobile. The swimming fish, floating jellyfish, swinging starfish, and shuffling sand dollar will keep your baby amused for hours.

Yarn

Knit Picks Mighty Stitch; medium weight #4; 80% acrylic, 20% superwash wool; 3.5 oz. (100 g)/208 yd. (190 m) per skein
- 1 skein each: 26814 Alfalfa, 26822 Conch, 26810 Canary, 26830 Sky, 26818 Blush, 26820 Silver, 26807 White

Hook and Other Materials
- US size F-5 (3.75 mm) crochet hook
- Yarn needle
- 10 in.(25.4 cm) wooden sewing hoop
- Poly-fil stuffing

Finished Measurements

Star: 3 in. (8 cm) wide
Sand Dollar: 3 in. (8 cm) wide
Fish: 4 in. (10 cm) wide
Shell: 4 in. (10 cm) wide
Jellyfish: 4 in. (10 cm) wide x 7 in. (18 cm) long
(including tentacles)

Gauge

10 sts x 11 rows = 2 in. (4 cm) in sc

Special Stitch

Single Crochet 2 Together (sc2tog). (Insert hook, yarn over, pull up loop) in each of the sts indicated, yarn over, draw through all loops on hook.

Pattern Notes
- When changing colors, complete the stitch until the last pull through; drop working yarn, pull through next color as last pull through to complete color change, and finish stitch.
- When working in the round, place marker in first stitch of round to indicate beginning of round.

INSTRUCTIONS

Shell (make 2)

With Blush, ch 7.

Row 1 (RS): Sc in second ch from hook and in each ch across, turn. (6 sts)

Row 2: Ch 1, sc in each st across, turn.

Row 3: Ch 1, 2 sc in first st, sc in next 4 sts, 2 sc in last st, turn. (8 sts)

Row 4: Ch 1, sc in next 2 sts, dc in next st, 2 dc in next 2 sts, dc in next st, sc in next 2 sts, turn. (10 sts)

Row 5: Ch 1, sc in first 2 sts, dc in next 2 sts, 2 dc in next 2 sts, dc in next 2 sts, sc in next 2 sts, turn. (12 sts)

Row 6: Ch 1, sc in next 2 sts, dc in next 3 sts, 2 dc in next 2 sts, dc in next 3 sts, sc in next 2 sts, turn. (14 sts)

Row 7: Ch 1, 2 sc in first st, sc in next st, dc in next 4 sts, 2 dc in next 2 sts, dc in next 4 sts, sc in next st, 2 sc in last st, turn. (18 sts)

Row 8: Ch 1, 2 sc in first st, sc in next st, dc in next 6 sts, 2 dc in next 2 sts, dc in next 6 sts, sc in next st, 2 sc in last st, turn. (22 sts) Fasten off.

Trim

Rnd 9: Ch 1, sc evenly across ends of rows, 3 sc in Row 1 stitch 1, sc 4 across Row 1, 3 sc in last st of Row 1, sc evenly across ends of rows and sl st to the first stitch in Row 8. Fasten off.

Detail

Using the photo as a guide, use Silver and sl st details onto each panel of Shell.

Finishing

With WS of Shell panels together, use yarn needle and Blush to sew together; stuff before closing.

Sand Dollar (make 2)

With White, Ch 2.

Rnd 1 (RS): 6 sc in second ch from hook, join with sl st in first sc. (6 sts)

Rnd 2: Ch 1, 2 sc in each st around, join with sl st in first sc. (12 sts)

Rnd 3: Ch 1, sc in joining st, 2 sc in next st, * sc in next st, 2 sc in next st, rep from * around, join with sl st in first sc. (18 sts)

Rnd 4: Ch 1, sc in joining st, sc in next st, 2 sc in next st, * sc in next 2 sts, 2 sc in next st, rep from * around, join with sl st in first sc. (24 sts)

Rnd 5: Ch 1, sc in joining st, sc in next 2 sts, 2 sc in next st, * sc in next 3 sts, 2 sc in next st, rep from * around, join with sl st in first sc. (30 sts)

Rnd 6: Ch 1, sc in joining st, sc in next 3 sts, 2 sc in next st, * sc in next 4 sts, 2 sc in next st, rep from * around, join with sl st in first sc. (36 sts)

Rnd 7: Ch 1, sc in joining st, sc in next 4 sts, 2 sc in next st * sc in next 5 sts, 2 sc in next st, rep from * around, join with sl st in first sc. (42 sts) Fasten off.

Detail

Using the photo as a guide, use Sky and stitch details onto each panel of the Sand Dollar.

Finishing

With WS of Sand Dollar panels together, use yarn needle and White to sew together; stuff before closing.

Starfish (make 2)

With Conch, ch 2.

Rnd 1: 5 sc in second ch from hook, join with sl st in first sc. (5 sts)

Rnd 2: Ch 1, 2 sc in each st from hook, join with sl st in first sc. (10 sts)

Rnd 3: Ch 1, sc in joining st, 2 sc in next st, * sc in next st, 2 sc in next st, rep from * around, join with sl st in first sc. (15 sts)

Rnd 4: Ch 1, sc in joining st, sc in next st, 2 sc in next st, * sc in next 2 sts, 2 sc in next st, rep from * around, join with sl st in first sc. (20 sts) Fasten off.

Points

Repeat the following pattern until you have 5 points:

Row 1 (RS): Join yarn in next st, ch 1, sc in next 4 sts, turn.

Rows 2–3: Ch 1, sc in each st across, turn.

Row 4: Sc2tog (see Special Stitch) twice. (2 sts)

Row 5: Sc2tog. (1 st) Fasten off.

Trim

Join in center between 2 Points, * sc 4 up Point, (sc, ch 1, sc) in tip, sc 4 down Point, rep from * around, join with sl st to first sc.

Finishing

With WS of Starfish panels together, use yarn needle and Conch to sew together; stuff before closing.

Fish

With Canary, ch 2.

Rnd 1: 4 sc in second ch from hook, join with sl st in first sc. (4 sts)

Rnd 2: Ch 1, 2 sc in each st around, join with sl st in first sc. (8 sts)

Rnd 3: Ch 1, sc in joining st, 2 sc in next st, * sc in next st, 2 sc in next st, rep from * around, join with sl st in first sc. (12 sts)

Rnd 4: Ch 1, sc in joining st, sc in next st, 2 sc in next st, * sc in next 2 sts, 2 sc in next st, rep from * around, join with sl st in first sc. (16 sts)

Rnd 5: Ch 1, sc in joining st, sc in next 2 sts, * sc in next 3 sts, 2 sc in next st, rep from * around, join with sl st in first sc. (20 sts)

Rnd 6: Ch 1, sc in joining st, sc in next 3 sts, * sc in next 4 sts, 2 sc in next st, rep from * around, join with sl st in first sc. (24 sts)

Rnds 7–8: Ch 1, sc in each st around, join with sl st in first st. Join White, fasten off Canary (see Pattern Notes).

Rnds 9–14: Ch 1, sc in each st around, join with sl st in first st.

Rnd 15: Sc2tog, sc in next 10 sts, sc2tog, sc in next 10 sts, join with sl st to first sc. (22 sts)

Rnd 16: Sc2tog, sc in next 9 sts, sc2tog, sc in next 9 sts, join with sl st to first sc. (20 sts)

Rnd 17: Sc2tog, sc in next 8 sts, sc2tog, sc in next 8 sts, join with sl st to first sc. (18 sts)

Rnd 18: Sc2tog, sc in next 7 sts, sc2tog, sc in next 7 sts, join with sl st to first sc. (16 sts)

Rnd 19: Sc2tog, sc in next 6 sts, sc2tog, sc in next 6 sts, join with sl st to first sc. (14 sts) Fasten off.

Fin

Fold with decreases on edges; lightly stuff body.

Row 1: Working through 2 loops of folded body as 1, sl st in edge, (ch 4, 2 tr) in first stitch, 2 tr in next st, (ch 2, sl st) in next st, (sl st, ch 2) in next st, 2 tr in next st, (2 tr, ch 4, sl st) in next st, sl st to edge. Fasten off.

Jellyfish

Top

With White, ch 2.

Rnd 1: 8 sc in second ch from hook, join with sl st to first sc. (8 sts)

Rnd 2: Ch 1, 2 sc in each st around, do not join. (16 sts)

Rnd 3: Working in the round (see Pattern Notes), (sc in next st, 2 sc in next st) around. (24 sts)

Rnd 4: (Sc in next 2 sts, 2 sc in next st) around. (32 sts)

Rnd 5: (Sc in next 3 sts, 2 sc in next st) around. (40 sts)

Rnd 6: (Sc in next 4 sts, 2 sc in next st) around. (48 sts)

Rnd 7: (Sc in next 5 sts, 2 sc in next st) around. (56 sts)

Rnds 8–12: Sc in each st around.

Rnd 13: (Sc2tog, sc in next 5 sts) around. (48 sts)

Rnds 14–15: Sc in each st around.

Rnd 16: (Sc2tog, sc in next 4 sts) around. Join Conch, fasten off White (see Pattern Notes). (40 sts)

Rnd 17: Ch 1, sc in each st around, join with sl st to first sc. Join White, fasten off Conch.

Rnd 18: Ch 1, sc in each st around, join with sl st to first sc. Fasten off.

Base

With Conch, ch 2.

Rnd 1: 8 sc in second ch from hook, join with sl st to first sc. (8 sts)

Rnd 2: Ch1, 2 sc in each st around, join with sl st to first sc. (16 sts)

Rnd 3: Ch 1, sc in joining st, 2 sc in next st, * sc in next st, 2 sc in next st, * rep from * around, join with sl st to first sc. (24 sts)

Rnd 4: Ch 1, sc in joining st, sc in next st, 2 sc in next st, * sc in next 2 sts, 2 sc in next st, rep from * around, join with sl st to first sc. (32 sts)

Rnd 5: Ch 1, sc in joining st, sc in next 2 sts, 2 sc in next st, * sc in next 3 sts, 2 sc in next st, rep from * around, join with sl st to first sc. (40 sts) Fasten off.

Tentacles

Short (make 3 each in White and Conch)

Ch 28.

Row 1: 3 sc in each ch across. Fasten off.

Long (make 3 in Canary)

Ch 36.

Row 1: 3 sc in each ch across. Fasten off.

Assembly

Attach Long Tentacles in center of Base. Attach Short Tentacles evenly around edge of Base.

Sew Base onto Top, stuffing before closing.

Seaweed Hangers (make 4)

With Alfalfa, ch 58.

Row 1: Dc in fourth ch from hook, dc in next 9 chs, 3 dc in next ch, * dc in next 10 chs, 3 dc in next ch, rep from * across. Fasten off.

Hoop Cover

With Sky, ch 8.

Rnd 1: Sc in second ch from hook and in each ch across, join with sl st to first sc. (7 sts)

Rnd 2: Ch 1, sc in each st around, do not join.

Rnds 3–175: Sc in each st around. Fasten off.

Slip onto hoop and sew ends together.

Mobile Assembly

Attach Seaweed Hangers evenly around the hoop.

Attach yarn to top of Shell, Sand Dollar, Starfish, and Fish. Attach evenly around hoop.

Pull all four ends of Seaweed Hangers to a point. Sew together with yarn needle.

Add yarn to top of Jellyfish, join at center of joining of Seaweed, and allow to drop in middle of hoop.

Finish

Join Alfalfa in joined Seaweed Hangers, ch 6, sl st to first ch, and join. Fasten off securely.

Sweet Dreams Sleepsack

Snuggle up your wee one in this adorable sleepsack. Made in one panel, this pattern is perfect for a quick on-the-go project.

Size
Newborn

Yarn
Knit Picks Brava; medium weight #4; 100% acrylic; 3.5 oz. (100 g)/218 yd. (199 m) per skein
- 2 skeins: 26362 Clarity

Hooks and Other Materials
- US size I-9 (5.5 mm) and H-8 (5 mm) crochet hooks
- Yarn needle
- Stitch markers
- 4 buttons (2 in./5 cm)
- Sewing needle and matching thread

Finished Measurements
12 in. (30 cm) wide x 21 in. (53 cm) long

Gauge
Using I-9 (5.5 mm) hook, 4 sts x 2 rows = 1 in. (2.5 cm) in dc

Special Stitches
Front Post Double Crochet (FPdc). Yarn over, insert hook from front to back around post of st indicated, yarn over and pull up a loop (3 loops on hook), (yarn over and draw through 2 loops on hook) twice.

Back Post Double Crochet (BPdc). Yarn over, insert hook from back to front around post of st indicated, yarn over and pull up a loop (3 loops on hook), (yarn over and draw through 2 loops on hook) twice.

Front Post Single Crochet (FPsc). Insert hook from front to back around post of st indicated, yarn over and pull up a loop (2 loops on hook), yarn over and draw through loops on hook.

Cluster (cl). Holding back last loop of each stitch on hook, 4 dc in stitch indicated, yarn over, pull through all loops on hook.

Pattern Note
- The beginning ch-2 of row will not count as a stitch.

INSTRUCTIONS

With I-9 (5.5 mm) hook, ch 53.

Row 1 (RS): Dc in fourth ch from hook and in each ch across, turn. (49 sts)

Row 2: Ch 3, * FPdc (see Special Stitches) on next post, BPdc (see Special Stitches) on next post, rep from * across, turn.

Row 3: Ch 3, * BPdc on next post, FPdc on next post, rep from * across, turn.

Row 4: Ch 1, FPsc (see Special Stitches) on each st across, turn.

Row 5: Ch 2 (see Pattern Note), dc in next 7 sts, * sc in next st, ch 3, cl (see Special Stitches) in next st, rep from * across until 7 sts remain, dc in last 7 sts, turn.

Rows 6–24: Ch 2, dc in next 7 sts, ch 3, cl in ch-3 sp, ch 1, rep from * across until 7 sts remain, dc in last 7 sts, turn.

Row 25: Ch 2, dc 2, sc in next st, ch 3, cl over next 4 sts, * sc in cl, ch 3, cl in ch-3 sp, ch 1, rep from * across until 7 sts remain, sc in next st, ch 3, cl over next 4 sts, ch 1, dc in last 2 sts, turn.

Rows 26–67: Ch 1, dc 2, * sc in cl, ch 3, cl in ch-3 sp, ch 1, rep from * across until 2 sts remain, dc in last 2 sts, turn.

Row 68: Ch 1, sc 2, * sk ch 1, sc in cl, 3 sc in ch 3, sc in sc, rep from * across until 2 sts remain, sc in last st. Fasten off, leaving a long end for sewing.

Hood

Fold Row 68 in half, use yarn needle and sew from front to back to form hood.

Trim

Rnd 1: With H-8 (5 mm) hook, join yarn on left edge of RS of Row 1, sc evenly across ends of rows, around hood, and sc evenly across ends of rows, sl st to first st of Row 1. Do not work across Row 1. Fasten off.

Finishing

Fold panel at Row 26 with WS facing. Mark WS of back behind Row 2 and Row 8 on each side with a stitch marker. This will be placement for buttons. Buttons will slip through dc stitches.

Use sewing needle and thread to attach buttons to WS.

Sweetcakes Stacker Rings

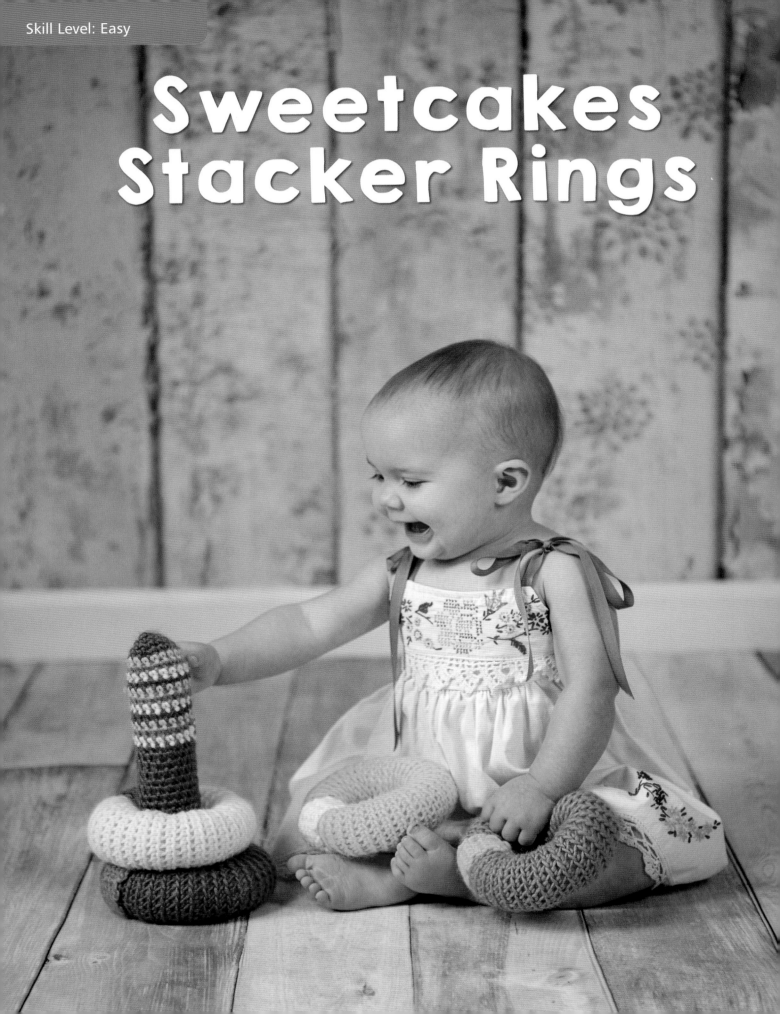

Keep little hands and minds busy with this colorful stacker ring set. It is not only fun to make but also an awesome way to use your extra yarn!

Yarn

Lion Brand Yarns New Basic 175 Yarn; medium weight #4; 75% acrylic, 25% wool; 3.5 oz. (100 g)/175 yd. (160 m) per skein

- 1 skein each: 147 Eggplant, 132 Mango, 172 Grass, 098 Cream

Hook and Other Materials

- US size 7 (4.5 mm) crochet hook
- Yarn needle
- Stitch markers
- Poly-fil stuffing

Finished Measurements

5½ in. (14 cm) wide x 9 in. (23 cm) high

Gauge

7 sts x 8 rows = 2 in. (5 cm) in sc

Special Stitch

Single Crochet 2 Together (sc2tog). (Insert hook, yarn over, pull up loop) in each of the sts indicated, yarn over, draw through all loops on hook.

Pattern Note

- When changing colors, complete the stitch until the last pull through; drop working yarn, pull through next color as last pull through to complete color change and finish stitch.

INSTRUCTIONS

Stacker Pole

With Eggplant, ch 2.

Rnd 1: 6 sc in second ch from hook, join with sl st to first sc. (6 sts)

Rnd 2: Ch 1, 2 sc in each st around, join with sl st to first sc. (12 sts)

Rnd 3: Ch 1, (sc in next st, 2 sc in next st) around, join with sl st to first sc. Join Mango, fasten off Eggplant (see Pattern Note). (18 sts)

Rnd 4: Ch 1, sc in each st around, join with sl st to first sc. Join Grass, fasten off Eggplant.

Rnd 5: Ch 1, sc in each st around, join with sl st to first sc. Join Cream, fasten off Grass.

Rnd 6: Ch 1, sc in each st around, join with sl st to first sc. Join Eggplant, fasten off Cream.

Rnd 7: Ch 1, sc in each st around, join with sl st to first sc. Join Grass, fasten off Eggplant.

Rnds 8–15: Rep Rnds 4–7; moving into Rnd 16, do not fasten off Eggplant.

Rnd 16: Ch 1, sc in each st around, do not join.

Rnds 17–35: Working in the round, sc in each st around.

Rnd 36: Working in the back loop only (blo), (sc in next st, sc2tog; see Special Stitch) around, join with sl st to first sc. (12 sts)

Stuff firmly before closing.

Rnd 37: Ch 1, working in both loops, sc2tog 6 times, join with sl st to first sc. (6 sts)

Rnd 38: Ch 1, sc in each st around, join with sl st to first sc. Fasten off, leaving long end for sewing.

Use yarn needle to close Rnd 38.

Rings

Eggplant

Ch 16, join with sl st to first ch.

Rnd 1: Ch 1, sc in each ch around, do not join. (16 sts)

Rnds 2–38: Working in the rnd, sc in each st around. To finish, sl st to first sc of last rnd.

Stuff firmly before sewing ends together.

Using yarn needle, sew ends together.

Mango

Ch 16, join with sl st to first ch.

Rnd 1: Ch 1, sc in each ch around, do not join. (16 sts)

Rnds 2–36: Working in the rnd, sc in each st around. To finish, sl st to first sc of last rnd.

Stuff firmly before sewing ends together.

Using yarn needle, sew ends together.

Grass

Ch 16, join with sl st to first ch.

Rnd 1: Ch 1, sc in each ch around, do not join. (16 sts)

Rnds 2–34: Working in the rnd, sc in each st around. To finish, sl st to first sc of last rnd.

Stuff firmly before sewing ends together.

Using yarn needle, sew ends together.

Cream

Ch 16, join with sl st to first ch.

Rnd 1: Ch 1, sc in each ch around, do not join. (16 sts)

Rnds 2–32: Working in the rnd, sc in each st around. To finish, sl st to first sc of last rnd.

Stuff firmly before sewing ends together.

Using yarn needle, sew ends together.

Tab

Make one in each color: Eggplant, Mango, Grass, Cream.

Ch 5.

Row 1: Sc in second ch from hook and in each across, turn. (4 sts)

Rows 2–16: Ch 1, sc in each st across, turn.

Use photo as guide for color placement, sew tab over seam of ring.

Finishing

Place Stacker Pole in Ring 1 (Eggplant) and use yarn needle to sew the 2 pieces together.

Cutie-Pie Stitch Sampler Blanket

This creative stitch sampler blanket is perfect for the crocheter who loves new stitches every other row. This is one project that is colorful, interesting to crochet, and even more fun to use!

Yarn

Plymouth Yarn Encore Worsted; medium weight #4; 75% acrylic, 25% wool; 3.5 oz (100 g)/200 yd. (183 m) per skein
- 1 skein each: 457 carnation, 449 Pink, 1201 Pale Green, 473 Aquarius, 801 Colonial Green, 9801 Dove, 208 White, 215 Yellow
- 2 skeins: 1317 Vacation Blues

Hook and Other Materials
- US size I-9 (5.5 mm) crochet hook
- Yarn needle
- Stitch markers

Finished Measurements

36 in. (91 cm) wide x 38 in. (97 cm) long

Gauge

16 sts x 8 rows = 4 in. (10 cm) in dc

Special Stitch

Cluster (cl). Holding back last loop of each stitch on hook, 2 dc in stitch indicated, yarn over, pull through all loops on hook.

Pattern Notes
- The beginning ch-5 of Round 1 counts as beginning ch, dc plus ch 1.
- The beginning ch-3 counts as the first dc.
- The beginning ch-6 counts as the first dc plus ch 3.
- When changing colors within the blanket, complete the stitch until the last pull through; drop working yarn, pull through next color as last pull through to complete color change and finish stitch.

INSTRUCTIONS

Motif (make 5)

Use photo as guide for Motif center colors.

Rnd 1 (RS): Ch 5, (dc, ch 1) in the first ch 11 times, join with sl st in ch-4 of beg ch-5. Fasten off.

Rnd 2: Join Color 2, ch 3, (yarn over, insert hook into ch-1 sp, pull up loop, yarn over, pull through first 2 loops on hook) twice, yarn over, pull through all loops on hook, ch 3 * cl in next ch-1 sp, ch 3, rep from * around, join with sl st to first cl. Fasten off.

Rnd 3: Join Vacation Blues in ch-3 sp, ch 1, sc in same ch-sp, ch 5, * sc in next ch-5 sp, ch 5, rep from * around, join with sl st in first sc. Fasten off.

Rnd 4: Join in any ch-5 sp, ch 3 (see Pattern Notes), (4 dc, ch 1, 5 dc) in same sp, *ch 1, sc in next ch-5 sp, ch 3, sc in next ch-5 sp, ch 1**, (5 dc, ch 1, 5 dc) in next ch-5 sp, rep from * around, ending last rep at **, join with sl st to beg ch-3. Fasten off.

Rnd 5: Join in corner ch-1 sp, ch 6 (see Pattern Notes), dc in same sp, * dc in next 5 sts, dc in next ch sp, dc in next sc, 3 dc in ch-3 sp, dc in next sc, dc in ch-2 sp, dc in next 5 dc **, (dc, ch 3, dc) in ch-1 sp, rep from * around, ending last rep at **, join with sl st to ch-3 of beg ch-6.

Rnd 6: Ch 1, sc in joining st, * 3 sc in ch-3 sp, sc in each st across, rep around, join with a sl st to first sc. Fasten off.

Use yarn needle to sew the 5 motifs together into one panel.

Side 1

Row 1: Join Pale Green in corner st right of RS of motif panel, ch 3, sk 2 sts, * 3 dc in next st, sk 2 sts, rep from * across, ending with dc in last stitch (opposite corner), turn. Join Carnation, fasten off Pale Green (see Pattern Notes).

Row 2: Ch 3, dc in same st, 3 dc between each 3 dc set across, ending with 2 dc in last st, turn. Join Yellow, fasten off Carnation.

Row 3: Ch 3, 3 dc between each 3 dc set across, ending with dc in last st, turn. Join Colonial Green, fasten off Yellow.

Row 4: Ch 3, dc in each st across, turn. Join Vacation Blues, fasten off Colonial Green.

Row 5: Ch 1, sl st in each st across, turn. Join Colonial Green, fasten off Vacation Blues.

Row 6: Using stitches from Row 4, ch 3, dc in each st across turn. Join White, fasten off Colonial Green.

Row 7: (*Note:* Work this row loosely.) Ch 1, sc, * ch 1, sk 1, sc in next st, rep from * across, turn. Join Pink, fasten off White.

Row 8: Ch 1, sc in first st, sc in next ch-1 sp, * ch 1, sc in next ch-1 sp, rep from * across until 1 st remains, sc in last st. Join Colonial Green, fasten off Pink.

Row 9: Ch 1, sc in first sc, ch 1, * sc in next ch-1 sp, ch 1, rep from * across, until 1 st remains, sc in last st, turn. Join Carnation, fasten off Colonial Green.

Row 10: Ch 1, rep Row 8. Join Yellow, fasten off Carnation.

Row 11: Ch 1, sc in first st, 2 sc in each ch-1 sp, sc in last st, turn. Join Pale Green, fasten off Yellow.

Row 12: Ch 5, 2 dc in same st, sk 2 sts, sl st in next st, * ch 3, 2 dc in same st, sk 2 sts, sl st in next st, rep from * across, turn. (39 peaks)

Row 13: Ch 4, 3 sc in top of each ch-3, sc in ch-3 of turning ch-5, turn. Join Vacation Blues, fasten off Pale Green.

Row 14: Ch 3, dc in each st across, turn. Join White, fasten off Vacation Blues.

Row 15: Ch 3, sk 2 sts, * (cl [see Special Stitch], ch 1, cl) in next st, sk 2 sts, rep from * across to last 2 sts, sk 1 st, dc in last st. (39 sets) Join Pink, fasten off White.

Row 16: Ch 1, sc in first st, ch 2, * sc in ch-1 sp, ch 2, rep from * across, ending with sc in last st. Join Yellow, fasten off Pink.

Row 17: Ch 3, dc in same st, sk ch sp, sk sc, 3 dc in each ch sp across to last ch sp, sk ch-sp, 2 dc in last st, turn. Join Dove, fasten off Yellow. (38 3-dc sets and 2 2-dc sets)

Row 18: Rep Row 8. Join Carnation, fasten off Dove.

Row 19: Rep Row 2. Join Pale Green, fasten off Carnation.

Rows 20–23: Rep Rows 4–6 (Color and Pattern), ending with Row 4. Join Yellow, fasten off Colonial Green.

Row 24: Rep Row 7. Join Vacation Blues, fasten off Yellow.

Row 25: Rep Row 8. Join Pale Green, fasten off Vacation Blues.

Row 26: Rep Row 9. Join Carnation, fasten off Pale Green.

Row 27: Rep Row 10. Join Pink, fasten off Carnation.

Row 28: Rep Row 11. Join White, fasten off Pink.

Row 29: Rep Row 12.

Row 30: Rep Row 13. Join Colonial Green, fasten off White.

Row 31: Rep Row 14. Join Yellow, fasten off Colonial Green.

Row 32: Rep Row 15. Join Vacation Blues, fasten off Yellow.

Row 33: Rep Row 16. Join Pink, fasten off Vacation Blues.

Row 34: Rep Row 17. Join Pale Green, fasten off Pink.

Row 35: Rep Row 18. Fasten off.

Side 2

Working on opposite side of motif panel, rep Rows 1–35 of Side 1.

Border

Rnd 1: Join Aquarius in the first st of Row 35, ch 1, 3 sc in same st, sc across to last st, 3 sc in last st, sc evenly across ends of rows as sts to Row 35 on Side 1, 3 sc in first st, sc across to last st, 3 sc in last st, sc evenly across ends of rows as sts, to first sc, join with sl st to first sc.

Rnd 2: Ch 1, sc in each st with 3 sc in second sc of 3-sc in corners, join with sl st to first sc. Join White, fasten off Aquarius.

Rnd 3: *Ch 3, sl st in next st, rep from * around, join with sl st to first sc. Fasten off.

Spun Sugar
Bonnet

This bonnet is as sweet as can be and perfect for any new baby girl!

Size
Newborn

Yarn
Red Heart Dreamy; bulky
weight #5; 100% acrylic;
8.8 oz. (250 g)/466 yd.
(426 m) per skein
• 1 skein: E861-8372 Rose

Hook and Other Materials
• US size F-5 (3.75 mm)
crochet hook
• Yarn needle

Finished Measurements
5½ in. (14 cm) wide x 5½ in.
(14 cm) long

Gauge
5 sts x 2 rows = 1 in. (2.5 cm)
in hdc

Special Stitch
Shell. (2 dc, ch 1, 2 dc) in
indicated stitch.

Pattern Note
• The beginning ch-6 counts as
the first treble plus ch 2.

INSTRUCTIONS

Ch 2.

Rnd 1: 10 hdc in first ch, join with sl st in first hdc. (10 sts)

Rnd 2: Ch 1, 2 hdc in each st around, join with sl st in first hdc. (20 sts)

Rnd 3: Ch 1, hdc in joining st, 2 hdc in next st, * hdc in next st, 2 hdc in next st, rep from * around, join with sl st in first hdc. (30 sts)

Rnd 4: Ch 1, hdc in joining st, hdc in next st, 2 hdc in next st, * hdc in next 2 sts, 2 hdc in next st, rep from * around, join with sl st in first hdc. (40 sts)

Rnd 5: Ch 1, hdc in joining st, hdc in next 2 sts, 2 hdc in next st, * hdc in next 3 sts, 2 hdc in next st, rep from * around, join with sl st in first hdc. (50 sts)

Row 6: Now working in rows, ch 1, sc in joining sc, * ch 5, sk 3 sts, sc in next st, rep from * across to last st, sc in last st, turn.

Row 7: Ch 6 (see Pattern Note), sc in first ch-5 loop, * shell (see Special Stitch) in next sc, sc in next ch-5 loop **, ch 5, sc in next ch-5 loop, rep from * across, ending last rep at **, ch 2, tr in last st, turn.

Row 8: Ch 1, sc in first st, * ch 5, sc in ch-1 sp of next shell, ch 5 **, sc in next ch-5 loop, rep from * across, ending last rep at **, sc in ch-3 of turning ch-6, turn.

Rows 9–14: Rep Rows 7 and 8.

Row 15: Ch 1, sc in first st, * (ch 1, sl st, ch 2, sl st, ch 2) in ch-sp **, sl st in next st, rep from * across, ending last rep at **, sc in last st. Fasten off.

Ties

Join in corner of Row 15, ch 46. Fasten off.
Rep on opposite side.

Birdie Lovie

This *"tweet"* lovie is the best first toy for babies to hug and hold. The little birdie can be made for any age, too!

Yarn

Cascade Yarns Pacific; medium weight #4; 60% acrylic, 40% superwash merino wool; 3.5 oz. (100 g)/213 yd. (195 m) per skein

- 1 skein each: 117 Semolina, 116 Lamb
- 1 skein: 110 Beach Glass

Hook and Other Materials

- US size F-5 (3.75 mm) crochet hook
- Yarn needle
- Stitch markers
- 2 safety eyes, 0.5 in. (12 mm)
- Poly-fil stuffing

Finished Measurements

Blanket: 13 in. (33 cm) wide x 13 in. (33 cm) long

Gauge

Using F-5 (3.75 mm) hook, 6 sts x 6 rows = 1 in. (2.5 cm) in sc

Special Stitch

Single Crochet 2 Together (sc2tog). Pull up a loop in each of next 2 sc, yarn over and draw through all 3 loops on hook (counts as 1 sc).

Pattern Notes

- Place marker in first stitch of round to indicate beginning of round.
- The beginning ch-3 counts as the first dc.
- When changing colors, complete the stitch until the last pull through; drop working yarn, pull through next color as last pull through to complete color change and finish stitch.

INSTRUCTIONS

Birdie

With F-5 (3.75 mm) hook and Beach Glass, ch 2.

Rnd 1: 7 sc in second ch from hook, do not join. (7 sts)

Rnd 2: Working in the round, 2 sc in each st around. (14 sts)

Rnd 3: (Sc in next st, 2 sc in next st) around. (21 sts)

Rnd 4: (Sc in next 2 sts, 2 sc in next st) around. (28 sts)

Rnd 5: (Sc in next 3 sts, 2 sc in next st) around. (35 sts)

Rnd 6: (Sc in next 4 sts, 2 sc in next st) around. (42 sts)

Rnd 7: (Sc in next 5 sts, 2 sc in next st) around. (49 sts)

Rnds 8–18: Sc in each st around.

Rnd 19: (Sc in next 5 sts, sc2tog [see Special Stitch]) around. (42 sts)

Rnd 20: (*Note:* Mark this rnd with stitch marker.) (Sc in next 4 sts, sc2tog) around. (35 sts)

Rnd 21: (Sc in next 4 sts, 2 sc in next st) around. (42 sts)

Rnds 22–27: Sc in each st around.

Add safety eyes in Rnd 20, 4 sts apart. Stitch on the Nose and detail line under eye.

Rnd 28: (Sc in next 4 sts, sc2tog) around. (35 sts)

Rnd 29: (Sc in next 3 sts, sc2tog) around. (28 sts)

Rnd 30: (Sc in next 2 sts, sc2tog) around. (21 sts)

Rnd 31: (Sc in next st, sc2tog) around. (14 sts) Stuff body firmly.

Rnd 32: Sc2tog 7 times. (7 sts)

Rnd 33: Sc in each st around, join with sl st to first st. Fasten off, leaving long end for sewing.

Use yarn needle and sew Rnd 33 together.

Wings (make 2)

With Beach Glass, ch 2.

Rnd 1: 7 sc in second ch from hook, join with sl st to first sc.

Rnd 2: Ch 1, 2 sc in each st around, join with sl st to first sc.

Rnds 3–4: Ch 1, sc in each st around, join with sl st to first sc. Lightly stuff wing.

Rnd 5: Sc2tog 7 times, join with sl st to first sc. Fasten off, leaving long end for sewing.

Lovie

With Semolina, ch 4, join with sl st to first ch to form ring.

Rnd 1: Ch 3 (see Pattern Notes), 2 dc in ring, ch 3, (3 dc in ring, ch 3) 3 times, join with sl st to beg ch-3.

Rnd 2: Sl st in next 2 sts, sl st into ch-3 sp, (ch 3, 2 dc, ch 3, 3 dc) in ch-3 sp, ch 1, * (3 dc, ch 3, 3 dc) in next ch-3 sp, ch 1, rep from * around, join with sl st to beg ch-3.

Rnd 3: Sl st in next 2 sts, sl st into ch-3 sp, (ch 3, 2 dc, ch 3, 3 dc) in ch-3 sp, ch 1, 3 dc in next ch-1 sp, ch 1, * (3 dc, ch 3, 3 dc) in next ch-3 sp, ch 1, 3 dc in next ch-1 sp, ch 1, rep from * around, join with sl st to beg ch-3.

Rnd 4: Sl st in next 2 sts, sl st into ch-3 sp, (ch 3, 2 dc, ch 3, 3 dc) in ch-3 sp, ch 1, (3 dc in next ch-1 sp, ch 1) twice, * (3 dc, ch 3, 3 dc) in next ch-3 sp, ch 1, (3 dc in next ch-1 sp, ch 1) twice, rep from * around, join with sl st to beg ch-3. Join Beach Glass, fasten off Semolina.

Rnd 5: Sl st in next 2 sts, sl st into ch-3 sp, (ch 3, 2 dc, ch 3, 3 dc) in ch-3 sp, ch 1, (3 dc in next ch-1 sp, ch 1) 3 times, * (3 dc, ch 3, 3 dc) in next ch-3 sp, ch 1, (3 dc in next ch-1 sp, ch 1) 3 times, rep from * around, join with sl st to beg ch-3. Join Semolina, fasten off Beach Glass.

Rnd 6: Sl st in next 2 sts, sl st into ch-3 sp, (ch 3, 2 dc, ch 3, 3 dc) in ch-3 sp, ch 1, (3 dc in next ch-1 sp, ch 1) 4 times, * (3 dc, ch 3, 3 dc) in next ch-3 sp, ch 1, (3 dc in next ch-1 sp, ch 1) 4 times, rep from * around, join with sl st to beg ch-3. Fasten off Semolina, join Lamb.

Rnd 7: Sl st in next 2 sts, sl st into ch-3 sp, (ch 3, 2 dc, ch 3, 3 dc) in ch-3 sp, ch 1, (3 dc in next ch-1 sp, ch 1) 5 times, * (3 dc, ch 3, 3 dc) in next ch-3 sp, ch 1, (3 dc in next ch-1 sp, ch 1) 5 times, rep from * around, join with sl st to beg ch-3. Join Semolina, fasten off Lamb.

Rnd 8: Sl st in next 2 sts, sl st into ch-3 sp, (ch 3, 2 dc, ch 3, 3 dc) in ch-3 sp, ch 1, (3 dc in next ch-1 sp, ch 1) 6 times, * (3 dc, ch 3, 3 dc) in next ch-3 sp, ch 1, (3 dc in next ch-1 sp, ch 1) 6 times, rep from * around, join with sl st to beg ch-3. Join Beach Glass, fasten off Semolina.

Rnd 9: Sl st in next 2 sts, sl st into ch-3 sp, (ch 3, 2 dc, ch 3, 3 dc) in ch-3 sp, ch 1, (3 dc in next ch-1 sp, ch 1) 7 times, * (3 dc, ch 3, 3 dc) in next ch-3 sp, ch 1, (3 dc in next ch-1 sp, ch 1) 7 times, rep from * around, join with sl st to beg ch-3. Join Semolina, fasten off Beach Glass.

Rnd 10: Sl st in next 2 sts, sl st into ch-3 sp, (ch 3, 2 dc, ch 3, 3 dc) in ch-3 sp, ch 1, (3 dc in next ch-1 sp, ch 1) 8 times, * (3 dc, ch 3, 3 dc) in next ch-3

sp, ch 1, (3 dc in next ch-1 sp, ch 1) 8 times, rep from * around, join with sl st to beg ch-3. Join Lamb, fasten off Semolina.

Rnd 11: Sl st in next 2 sts, sl st into ch-3 sp, (ch 3, 2 dc, ch 3, 3 dc) in ch-3 sp, ch 1, (3 dc in next ch-1 sp, ch 1) 9 times, * (3 dc, ch 3, 3 dc) in next ch-3 sp, ch 1, (3 dc in next ch-1 sp, ch 1) 9 times, rep from * around, join with sl st to beg ch-3. Join Semolina, fasten off Lamb.

Rnd 12: Sl st in next 2 sts, sl st into ch-3 sp, (ch 3, 2 dc, ch 3, 3 dc) in ch-3 sp, ch 1, (3 dc in next ch-1 sp, ch 1) 10 times, * (3 dc, ch 3, 3 dc) in next ch-3 sp, ch 1, (3 dc in next ch-1 sp, ch 1) 10 times, rep from * around, join with sl st to beg ch-3. Join Beach Glass, fasten off Semolina.

Rnd 13: Ch 1, sc in joining st, sc in next 2 sts, 3 sc in ch-3 sp, * sc in each st and ch-1 sp ** to next ch-3 sp, 3 sc in ch-3 sp, rep from * around, ending last rep at **, sl st to first sc to join. Fasten off Beach Glass, join Semolina.

Rnd 14: Ch 1, sc in each st to second st of 3 sc in corner, * 3 sc in second sc, sc in each st to corner rep from * around, ending with sl st to first sc. Fasten off.

Finishing

Use yarn needle to sew the bottom of the Birdie onto the center of Lovie.

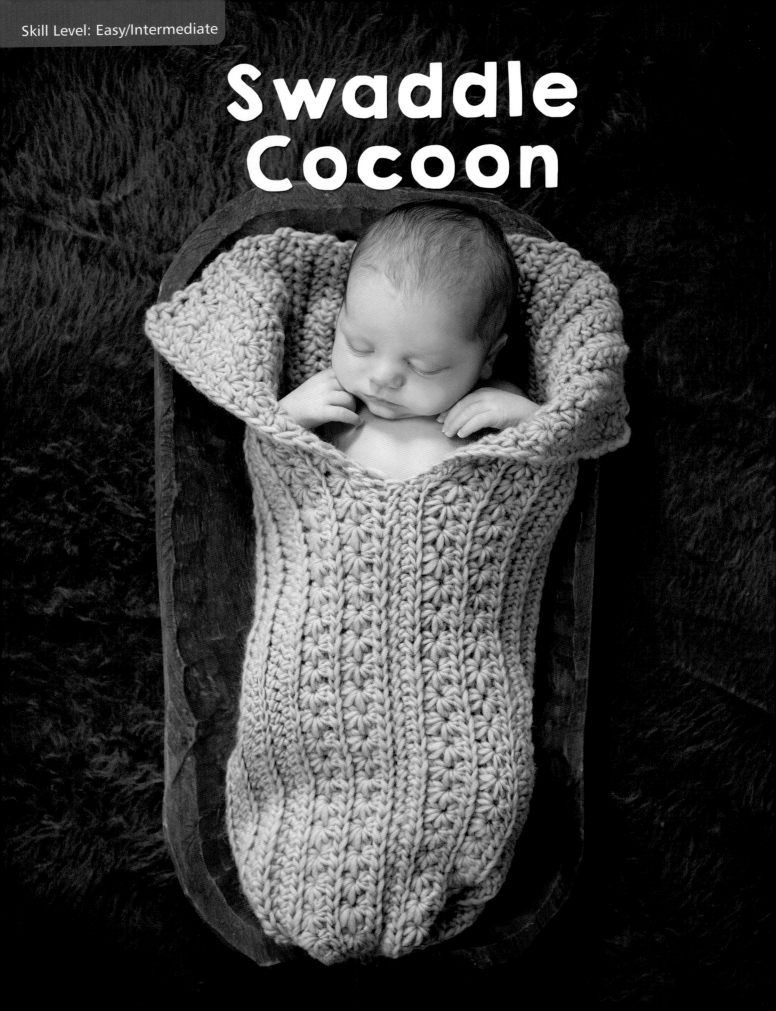

Swaddle Cocoon

Create a cuddly baby cocoon that is oh-so-adorable and photo worthy for your baby.

Size
Newborn

Yarn
Patons Roving Wool; bulky weight #5; 100% pure new wool; 3.5 oz. (100 g)/120 yd. (109 m) per skein
- 3 skeins: 241077 Natural

Hook and Other Materials
- US size K-10½ (6.5 mm) crochet hook
- Yarn needle

Finished Measurements
9 in. (23 cm) wide x 21 in. (54 cm) long

Gauge
3 sts x 2 rows = 1 in. (10 cm) in hdc

Special Stitch
Star Stitch. The star stitch has a special first stitch, but the remaining stitches are the same.

First stitch: Ch 3, insert hook into the second ch from the hook and pull up a loop. Then do the same in the third chain and then the base stitch, insert hook into the next stitch, pull up a loop. This leaves you with 5 loops on the hook. Do not pull loops tight—keep loose.

Yarn over and pull through all 5 loops. Ch 1 to finish off the stitch. First Star made.

Each star to end of row: * Insert the hook into the ch 1 just made, and pull up a loop. Insert the hook into the same stitch that the last star stitch was in, yarn over and pull back a loop. Keep all loops on hook. Insert hook into the next st, yarn over and pull back loop. Insert hook into next stitch and pull up loop. This leaves you with 5 loops on hook; do not pull tight. Yarn over, pull through all loops, ch 1 to finish the stitch.

Pattern Note
- The cocoon is made in one panel, sewn two-thirds of the way and then closed at one end to finish.

INSTRUCTIONS

Ch 59.

Row 1 (WS): Hdc in second ch from hook and in each ch across, turn. (59 sts)

Row 2: Working in the back loop only (blo), star stitch (see Special Stitch) across, dc in last st, turn. (59 sts)

Row 3: Ch 2, 2 hdc in each ch-sp across, hdc in last st, turn. (60 sts)

Row 4: Rep Row 2.

Row 5: Rep Row 3.

Row 6: Ch 2, working in blo, hdc in each st across, turn.

Row 7: Ch 1, hdc in each st across, turn.

Rows 8–33: Rep Rows 6 and 7.

Rows 34–37: Rep Rows 2 and 3. Fasten off.

Use yarn needle, starting at one end (bottom) and sew two-thirds together, leaving remaining sts unworked.

Closing Bottom of Cocoon

Turn piece wrong side out. Using scrap piece of yarn, pins, or split ring markers, place 8 markers evenly spaced around bottom edge that has already been sewn together. Thread yarn needle with long length of yarn. Sew bottom closed by stitching together in a star pattern, working opposite edges and pulling in corners.

Cuddle Me Stroller Blanket

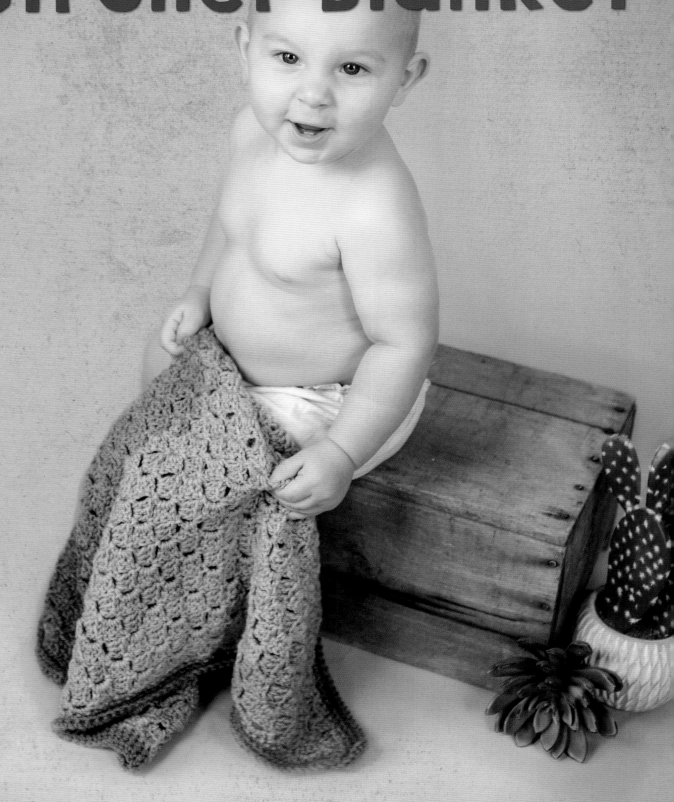

Protect your baby from any weather with this easy-to-crochet car seat cover. It is worked corner to corner, and it is amazing to watch it come together when using an ombre or self-striping yarn.

Yarn

Lion Brand Yarns Cupcake; light weight #3; 100% acrylic; 5.3 oz. (150 g)/590 yds. (540 m) per skein
• 2 skeins: 222 Tundra

Hook

US size H-8 (5 mm) crochet hook

Finished Measurements

22 in. (56 cm) wide x 22 in. (56 cm) long

Gauge

4 sts x 5 rows = 1 in. (2.5 cm) in sc

Pattern Note

• The blanket is made in a corner-to-corner stitch (see instructions for how to work).

INSTRUCTIONS

Row 1: Ch 6, dc in the 4th ch from hook and in next 2 ch (1 block made).

Row 2: Ch 6, turn, dc in 4th ch from hook and in next 2 ch, (sl st, ch 3, 3 dc) in ch-3 sp of previous row (2 blocks made).

Row 3: Ch 6, turn, dc in 4th ch from hook and in next 2 ch, [(sl st, ch 3, 3 dc) in next ch-3 sp of previous row] twice (3 blocks made).

Row 4: Ch 6, turn, dc in 4th ch from hook and in next 2 ch, [(sl st, ch 3, 3 dc) in next ch-3 sp of previous row] 3 times (4 blocks made).

Rows 5–28: Continue in this manner, increasing 1 block on each row until there are 29 blocks on middle row.

Begin decreasing rows as follows:

Row 29: Sl st across first 3 dc, *(sl st, ch 3, 3 dc) in next ch-3 sp of previous row; rep from * to last ch-3 sp, sl st in last sp, turn, do not make a block in last space (27 blocks).

Rep Row 29 until 1 block rem. Fasten off.

Border

There are two sections around the edge: a ch-3 (or dc edge) and a 3 dc.

Row 1: Join yarn in ch-3 sp in any corner, 2 sc in ch-3 sp, sc in each dc across the 3-dc section. Do not do anything in corners. Just work in each sp, sl st to first st to join.

Row 2: Ch 3, *dc in each st to corner (there will be a natural corner created from Row 1), 3 dc in corner; rep from * around, sl st to first st to join. Fasten off.

Wiggle Bum
Diaper Cover

and Headband Set

Adorably buttoned, this baby diaper cover will be a hit at any baby shower. Leave off the flower to have the perfect diaper cover for your baby boy, too. The headband works up quickly and is easy to adjust for any girl in the family.

Sizes
0–6 months, 6–12 months

Yarn
Knit Picks Swish Worsted; medium weight #4; 100% superwash merino wool; 1.76 oz. (50 g)/110 yd. (101 m) per skein
- 3 skeins: 24090 Squirrel Heather
- 1 skein: 25147 Amethyst Heather

Hook and Other Materials
- US size F-5 (3.75 mm) crochet hook
- Yarn needle
- 1 button (1 in./2.5 cm)
- Sewing needle and matching thread

Finished Measurements
Diaper Cover finished and buttoned:
0–6 months: 6 in. (15 cm) wide (strap) x 15 in. (38 cm) long
6–12 months: 7 in. (15 cm) wide (strap) x 16 in. (40.6 cm) long
Headband, adjustable by ties

Gauge
5 sts x 3 rows = 1 in. (2.5 cm) in dc

Special Stitches
Double Crochet 2 Together (dc2tog). Yarn over, pull up a loop in next st, yarn over, pull through first 2 loops, yarn over, pull up a loop in the next stitch, yarn over and draw through first 2 loops, yarn over, pull through all loops on hook (counts as 1 dc).
Single Crochet 2 Together (sc2tog). (Insert hook, yarn over, pull up loop) in each of the sts indicated, yarn over, draw through all loops on hook.

Pattern Note
- The beginning ch-3 of row will count as the first dc.

INSTRUCTIONS

Diaper Cover

0–6 months

With Squirrel Heather, ch 77.

Row 1: Sc in second ch from hook and in each across, turn. (76 sts)

Row 2: Ch 3, dc in each st across, turn.

Row 3: Ch 1, sc 3, ch 4, sk 4, sc to last 7 sts, ch 4, sk 4, sc in last 3 sts, turn. (2 buttonholes made)

Row 4: Ch 3, dc 3, dc in each of the next 4 chs, dc to next ch-4 sp, dc in each of next 4 chs, dc in last 3 sts, turn.

Row 5: Ch 1, sc in each st across, turn.

Row 6: Sl st in next 15 sts, ch 3, dc until 14 sts remain, leave remaining sts unworked, turn. (48 sts)

Row 7: Ch 1, sc in each st across, turn.

Row 8: Ch 3, dc2tog (see Special Stitches), dc to last 3 sts, dc2tog, dc in last st, turn. (46 sts)

Row 9: Ch 1, sc in first st, sc2tog (see Special Stitches), sc to last 3 sts, sc2tog, sc in last st, turn. (44 sts)

Row 10: Ch 3, dc2tog, dc to last 3 sts, dc2tog, dc in last st, turn. (42 sts)

Row 11: Ch 1, sc in first st, sc2tog, sc to last 3 sts, sc2tog, sc in last st, turn. (40 sts)

Row 12: Ch 3, dc2tog, dc to last 3 sts, dc2tog, dc in last st, turn. (38 sts)

Row 13: Ch 1, sc in first st, sc2tog, sc to last 3 sts, sc2tog, sc in last st, turn. (36 sts)

Row 14: Ch 3, dc2tog, dc to last 3 sts, dc2tog, dc in last st, turn. (34 sts)

Row 15: Ch 1, sc in first st, sc2tog, sc to last 3 sts, sc2tog, sc in last st, turn. (32 sts)

Row 16: Ch 3, dc in each st across, turn.

Row 17: Ch 1, sc in each st across, turn.

Rows 18–44: Rep Rows 16 and 17.

Trim

Rnd 1: Ch 1, 3 sc in the first st, sc to last st of Row 44, 3 sc in last st, sc evenly across ends of rows until the bottom corner of the strap, 3 sc in corner, sc evenly across ends of rows to Row 1, 3 sc in first st, sc across Row 1, 3 sc in last st, sc evenly across ends of rows to bottom of strap, 3 sc in corner, sc evenly across ends of rows until Row 44, join with sl st to first sc. Fasten off.

Sew button onto RS in middle front, slip buttonholes over button.

6–12 months

Using Squirrel Heather, ch 85.

Row 1: Sc in second ch from hook and in each across, turn. (84 sts)

Row 2: Ch 3, dc in each st across, turn.

Row 3: Ch 1, sc 3, ch 4, sk 4, sc to last 7 sts, ch 4, sk 4, sc in last 3 sts, turn. (2 buttonholes made)

Row 4: Ch 3, dc 3, dc in each of the next 4 chs, dc to next ch-4 sp, dc in each of next 4 chs, dc in last 3 sts, turn.

Row 5: Ch 1, sc in each st across, turn.

Row 6: Sl st in next 15 sts, ch 3, dc until 14 sts remain, leave remaining sts unworked, turn. (54 sts)

Row 7: Ch 1, sc in each st across, turn.

Row 8: Ch 3, dc2tog (see Special Stitches), dc to last 3 sts, dc2tog, dc in last st, turn. (52 sts)

Row 9: Ch 1, sc in first st, sc2tog (see Special Stitches), sc to last 3 sts, sc2tog, sc in last st, turn. (50 sts)

Row 10: Ch 3, dc2tog, dc to last 3 sts, dc2tog, dc in last st, turn. (48 sts)

Row 11: Ch 1, sc in first st, sc2tog, sc to last 3 sts, sc2tog, sc in last st, turn. (46 sts)

Row 12: Ch 3, dc2tog, dc to last 3 sts, dc2tog, dc in last st, turn. (44 sts)

Row 13: Ch 1, sc in first st, sc2tog, sc to last 3 sts, sc2tog, sc in last st, turn. (42 sts)

Row 14: Ch 3, dc2tog, dc to last 3 sts, dc2tog, dc in last st, turn. (40 sts)

Row 15: Ch 1, sc in first st, sc2tog, sc to last 3 sts, sc2tog, sc in last st, turn. (38 sts)

Row 16: Ch 3, dc2tog, dc to last 3 sts, dc2tog, dc in last st, turn. (36 sts)

Row 17: Ch 1, sc in first st, sc2tog, sc to last 3 sts, sc2tog, sc in last st, turn. (34 sts)

Row 18: Ch 3, dc in each st across, turn.

Row 19: Ch 1, sc in each st across, turn.

Rows 20–48: Rep Rows 18 and 19.

Trim

Rnd 1: Ch 1, 3 sc in the first st, sc to last st of Row 48, 3 sc in last st, sc evenly across ends of rows until the bottom corner of the strap, 3 sc in corner, sc evenly across ends of rows to Row 1, 3 sc in first st, sc across Row 1, 3 sc in last st, sc evenly across ends of rows to bottom of strap, 3 sc in corner, sc evenly across ends of rows until Row 48, join with sl st to first sc. Fasten off.

Sew button onto RS in middle front, slip buttonholes over button.

Flower

With Amethyst Heather, ch 8, join to first ch to create ring.

Rnd 1 (RS): Ch 1, 16 sc in ring, join with sl st to first sc. (16 sts)

Rnd 2: Ch 1, sc in same st, ch 3, sk 1, * sc in next st, ch 3, sk 1, rep from * around, join with sl st in first sc. (8 ch-3 sp, 8 sc)

Rnd 3: (Sl st, ch 1, 5 dc, ch 1, sl st) in each ch-3 sp, join with sl st in first sl st.

Rnd 4: Ch 1, sc in next st, working behind petals, * ch 5 sc in next sc, rep from around, join with sl st in first sc.

Rnd 5: (Sl st, ch 1, dc, 5 tr, dc, ch 1, sl st) in each ch-5 sp, join with sl st in first sl st. Fasten off.

Slip flower over button to finish.

Headband (all sizes)

With Squirrel Heather, ch 67.

Row 1: Ch 1, sc in first st, *ch 3, sk 1, sc in next st, rep from * across, ch 3, working in free loops of beginning ch, sc in first ch, [ch 3, sk 1, sc in next ch] across to last ch 3, sk 1, sl st in first sc to join.

Ties

Join yarn on edge of headband, ch 46. Fasten off. Repeat on opposite side.

Tip: To make the ties longer for older children, increase the Tie chains by 20.

Tie headband and adjust as needed to fit child.

Securely sew button off center of headband where flower placement will be.

Flower

With Amethyst Heather, ch 8, join to first ch to create ring.

Rnd 1 (RS): Ch 1, 16 sc in ring, join with sl st to first sc. (16 sts)

Rnd 2: Ch 1, sc in same st, ch 3, sk 1, * sc in next st, ch 3, sk 1, rep from * around, join with sl st in first sc. (8 ch-3 sp, 8 sc)

Rnd 3: (Sl st, ch 1, 5 dc, ch 1, sl st) in each ch-3 sp, join with sl st in first sl st.

Slip flower over button.

Dazzle Beanie

There's no need to wait for a garden party to wear this hat and bring out the pearls! Crochet this beauty in every color!

Sizes
3–6 months, 9–12 months

Yarn
Plymouth Yarn Encore Worsted; medium weight #4; 75% acrylic, 25% wool; 3.5 oz. (100 g)/200 yd. (183 m) per skein
• 1 skein each: 449 Pink, 1201 Pale Green, 9801 Dove

Hook and Other Materials
• US size F-5 (3.75 mm) crochet hook for 3–6 month size; US size H-8 (5 mm) crochet hook for 9–12 month size
• Yarn needle

Finished Measurements
3–6 months
Circumference: 14–16 in. (36–41 cm)
Hat height: 5.5 in. (14 cm)
9–12 months
Circumference: 16–18 in. (36–46 cm)

Gauge
With F-5 (3.75 mm) hook, 5 sts x 3 rows = 1 in. (2.5 cm) in dc; with H-8 (5 mm) hook, 4 sts x 2 rows = 1 in. (2.5 cm) in dc

Special Stitches
Beginning Cluster (beg cl). Ch 2, (yarn over, pull up loop, yarn over, pull through first 2 loops) twice in same ch sp.
Cluster (cl). Holding back last loop of each stitch on hook, 3 dc in stitch indicated, yarn over, pull through all loops on hook.
Shell. 5 dc in indicated stitch or space.

Pattern Notes
• The beginning ch-3 counts as the first double crochet.
• The beginning ch-5 counts as the first dc plus ch 2.
• When changing colors, complete the stitch until the last pull through; drop working yarn, pull through next color as last pull through to complete color change and finish stitch.
• To make the 9–12 month size, use an H-8 (5 mm) crochet hook, and it will increase the size naturally.

INSTRUCTIONS

Note: The instructions are the same for both sizes; use the F-5 hook for 3–6 months or H-8 for 9–12 months.

With Pale Green, ch 2.

Rnd 1: 8 sc in second ch from hook, join with sl st to first sc. (8 sts)

Rnd 2: Ch 3 (see Pattern Notes), dc in same st, 2 dc in each st around, join with sl st to beg ch-3. (16 sts)

Rnd 3: Ch 1, sc in same st, ch 3, sk 1 st, * sc in next st, ch 3, sk 1 st, rep from * around, join with sl st to first sc.

Rnd 4: Sl st to next ch-sp, beg cl (see Special Stitches), ch 4, * cl (see Special Stitches) in next ch-sp, ch 4, rep from * around, join with sl st to top of beg cl.

Rnd 5: Ch 1, (sc, ch 3, sc) in same st, * ch 3, sc over ch and in Rnd 3 sc, ch 3 **, (sc, ch 3, sc) in top of cluster, rep from * ending last rep at **, join with sl st to first sc.

Rnd 6: Sl st to next ch-3 sp, ch 1, sc in ch-3 sp, * ch 4, dc in sc, ch 4, sk ch-3 **, sc in ch-3 sp at top of cl, sk sc and ch-3, rep from * ending last rep at **, join with sl st in first sc.

Rnd 7: Ch 1, sc in same st, 4 sc in ch-4 sp, * ch 1, sk 1 st, 4 sc in next ch-4 sp, rep from * around, join with sl st in first sc.

Rnd 8: Ch 3, 4 dc in same st, shell (see Special Stitches) in each ch-1 sp around, join with sl st in beg ch-3.

Rnd 9: Ch 5 (see Pattern Notes), dc in sp between shells, sc in third dc of shell, * (dc, ch 2, dc) in sp between next 2 shells, sc in third dc of next shell, rep from * around, join with sl st to ch-3 of beg ch-5.

Rnd 10: Sl st to next ch-2 sp, ch3, 4 dc in same sp, shell in each ch-2 sp around, join with sl st to beg ch-3.

Rnds 11–17: Rep Rnds 9 and 10, ending on Rnd 9. Join Dove, fasten off Pale Green.

Rnd 18: Ch 1, sc in same st, 2 sc in ch-2 sp, sc in next dc, sc in sc, * sc in next dc, 2 sc in ch-2 sp, sc in next dc, sc in next sc, rep from * around, join with sl st to first sc.

Rnd 19: Ch 1, sc in each st around, join with sl st to first sc.

Rnd 20: Ch 1, *sc 14, sc2tog (see Special Stitches) rep from * around, join with sl st to first sc. Join Pale Green, fasten off Dove. (75 sts)

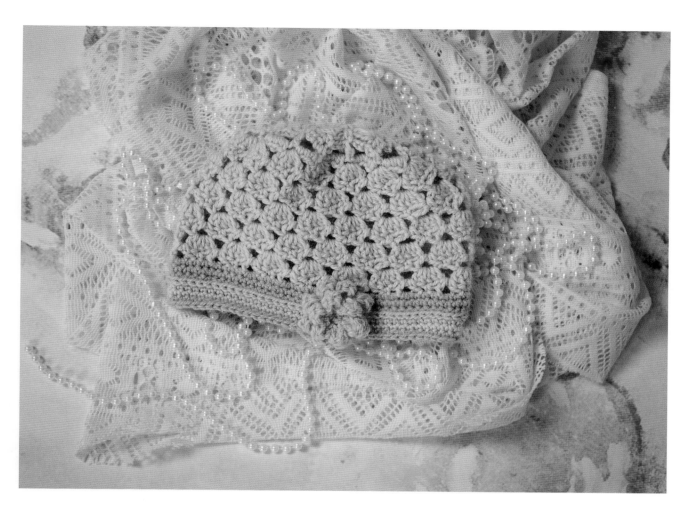

Rnds 21–22: Ch 1, sc in each st around. Join Dove, fasten off Pale Green.

Rnd 23: Ch 1, sc in each st around. Fasten off.

Detail

Join Pink in Rnd 20 at sl st join, ch 1, loosely sl st on the posts between Rows 19 and 20 to embellish. Sl st to first sl st to join. Fasten off.

Flower
Front

With Pink, ch 2.

Rnd 1: 6 sc in second ch from hook, join with sl st to first sc. (6 sc)

Rnd 2: (Sl st, ch 1, dc, tr, dc, ch 1, sl st) in each st around, join with sl st to first sc. (6 petals) Fasten off.

Back

With Pink, ch 4.

Rnd 1: 8 dc in first ch, join with sl st to first dc. (8 dc)

Rnd 2: (Sl st, ch 1, dc, tr, dc, ch 1, sl st) in each st around, join with sl st to first sc. (8 petals) Fasten off.

Snuggle Bunny

This bunny is sure to please all the little ones in your family. Mix and match colors to personalize your own floppy-ear snuggle bunny.

Yarn

Red Heart Dreamy; bulky weight #5; 100% acrylic; 8.8 oz. (250 g)/466 yd. (426 m) per skein
- 1 skein each: 8372 Rose (scrap yarn for bow only), 8331 Ivory, 8341 Gray

Hook and Other Materials
- US size G-6 (4 mm) crochet hook
- Yarn needle
- Stitch markers
- 2 safety eyes, 0.5 in. (12 mm)

Finished Measurements

11 in. (28 cm) high

Gauge

16 sts x 16 rows = 4 in. (10 cm) in sc

Special Stitch

Single Crochet 2 Together (sc2tog). Pull up a loop in each of next 2 sc, yarn over and draw through all 3 loops on hook (counts as 1 sc).

Pattern Note
- When changing colors, complete the stitch until the last pull through; drop working yarn, pull through next color as last pull through to complete color change and finish stitch.

INSTRUCTIONS

With Gray, ch 2.

Rnd 1: 6 sc in second ch from hook, join with sl st to first sc. (6 sts)

Rnd 2: Ch 1, 2 sc in each st, join with sl st to first sc. (12 sc) Join Ivory, drop Gray (see Pattern Note).

Rnd 3: Ch 1, sc in first st, 2 sc in next st, * sc in next st, 2 sc in next st, rep from * around, join with sl st to first sc. (18 sts)

Rnd 4: Ch 1, sc in first st, sc in next st, 2 sc in next st, * sc in next 2 sts, 2 sc in next st, rep from * around, join with sl st to first sc. Pick up Gray, drop Ivory. (24 sts)

Rnd 5: Ch 1, sc in first st, sc in next 2 sts, 2 sc in next st, * sc in next 3 sts, 2 sc in next st, rep from * around, join with sl st to first st. (30 sts)

Rnd 6: Ch 1, sc in first st, sc in next 3 sts, 2 sc in next st, * sc in next 4 sts, 2 sc in next st, rep from * around, join with sl st to first st. Pick up Ivory, drop Gray. (36 sts)

Rnd 7: Ch 1, sc in first st, sc in next 4 sts, 2 sc in next st, * sc in next 5 sts, 2 sc in next st, rep from * around, join with sl st to first st. (42 sts)

Rnd 8: Ch 1, sc in first st, sc in next 5 sts, 2 sc in next st, * sc in next 6 sts, 2 sc in next st, rep from * around, join with sl st to first st. Pick up Gray, drop Ivory. (48 sts)

Rnds 9–10: Ch 1, sc in each st, join with sl st to first st. Pick up Ivory, drop Gray.

Rnds 11–12: Ch 1, sc in each st, join with sl st to first st. Pick up Gray, drop Ivory.

Rnds 13–27: Rep Rnds 9–12, ending with Rnd 11.

Rnd 28: Continuing with Ivory, ch 1, sc in first st, sc in next 5 sts, sc2tog (see Special Stitch), * sc in next 6 sts, sc2tog, rep from * around, join with sl st to first st. Pick up Gray, drop Ivory. (42 sts)

Rnd 29: Ch 1, sc in each st around, join with a sl st to first st.

Rnd 30: Ch 1, sc in first st, sc in next 4 sts, sc2tog, * sc in next 5 sts, sc2tog, rep from * around, join with sl st to first st. Pick up Ivory, drop Gray. (36 sts)

Rnd 31: Ch 1, sc in each st around, join with a sl st to first st.

Rnd 32: Ch 1, sc in first st, sc in next 3 sts, sc2tog, * sc in next 4 sts, sc2tog, rep from * around, join with sl st to first st. Pick up Gray, drop Ivory. (30 sts)

Rnd 33: Ch 1, sc in first st, sc in next 2 sts, sc2tog, * sc in next 3 sts, sc2tog, rep from * around, join with sl st to first st. (24 sts)

Rnd 34: Ch 1, sc in first st, sc in next st, sc2tog, * sc in next 2 sts, sc2tog, rep from * around, join with sl st to first st. Pick up Ivory, fasten off Gray. (18 sts) Stuff body firmly.

Rnd 35: Ch 1, sc in each st around, join with sl st to first st.

Rnd 36: Ch 1, sc in first st, sc in next st, 2 sc in next st, * sc in next 2 sts, 2 sc in next st, rep from * around, do not join. (24 sts)

Rnd 37: Working in the round, * sc in next 3 sts, 2 sc in next st, rep from * around. (30 sts)

Rnd 38: * Sc in next 4 sts, 2 sc in next st, rep from * around. (36 sts)

Rnd 39: * Sc in next 5 sts, 2 sc in next st, rep from * around. (42 sts)

Rnds 40–49: (*Note:* Mark Rnd 47 with stitch marker.) Sc in each st around.

Rnd 50: * Sc in next 5 sts, sc2tog, rep from * around. (36 sts)

Rnd 51: * Sc in next 4 sts, sc2tog, rep from * around. (30 sts)

Rnd 52: * Sc in next 3 sts, sc2tog, rep from * around. (24 sts)

Add safety eyes in Rnd 47. Stitch on Nose. Stuff head firmly.

Rnd 53: * Sc in next 2 sts, sc2tog, rep from * around. (18 sts)

Rnd 54: * Sc in next st, sc2tog, rep from * around. (12 sts)

Rnd 55: Sc2tog 6 times.

Rnd 56: Sc in each st around, sl st to the first st to join. Fasten off, leaving a long end for sewing.

Use yarn needle to close Rnd 56.

Ears (make 2)

With Ivory, ch 2.

Rnd 1: 8 sc in second ch from hook, do not join. (8 sts)

Rnd 2: Working in the round, 2 sc in each st around. (16 sts)

Rnd 3: * Sc in next st, 2 sc in next st, rep from * around. (24 sts)

Rnd 4: * Sc in next 2 sts, 2 sc in next st, rep from * around. (32 sts)

Rnds 5–8: Sc in each st around.

Rnd 9: Sc2tog, sc in next 14 sts, sc2tog, sc in next 14 sts. (30 sts)

Rnd 10: Sc in each st around.

Rnd 11: Sc2tog, sc in next 13 sts, sc2tog, sc in next 13 sts. (28 sts)

Rnd 12: Sc in each st around.

Rnd 13: Sc2tog, sc in next 12 sts, sc2tog, sc in next 12 sts. (26 sts)

Rnd 14: Sc in each st around.

Rnd 15: Sc2tog, sc in next 11 sts, sc2tog, sc in next 11 sts. (24 sts)

Rnd 16: Sc in each st around.

Rnd 17: Sc2tog, sc in next 10 sts, sc2tog, sc in next 10 sts. (22 sts)

Rnd 18: Sc in each st around.

Rnd 19: Sc2tog, sc in next 9 sts, sc2tog, sc in next 9 sts. (20 sts)

Rnd 20: Sc in each st around.

Rnd 21: Sc2tog, sc in next 8 sts, sc2tog, sc in next 8 sts. (18 sts)

Rnd 22: Sc in each st around.

Rnd 23: Sc2tog, sc in next 7 sts, sc2tog, sc in next 7 sts. (16 sts)

Rnd 24: Sc in each st around.

Rnd 25: Sc2tog, sc in next 6 sts, sc2tog, sc in next 6 sts. (14 sts)

Rnd 26: Sc in each st around.

Rnd 27: Sc2tog, sc in next 5 sts, sc2tog, sc in next 5 sts. (12 sts)

Rnd 28: Sc in each st around.

Rnd 29: Sc2tog, sc in next 4 sts, sc2tog, sc in next 4 sts. (10 sts)

Rnds 30–32: Sc in each st around, join with sl st to first st. Fasten off, leaving long end for sewing.

Finishing
With yarn needle, sew ears to top of head. Tie bow in Rose in center.

Lil' Boss Pullover

This cute little sweater is worked with a fun stitch and made in one panel. You'll be amazed at how easy it is to crochet and how cute it is to wear!

Sizes
3–6 months, 9–12 months

Yarn
Knit Picks City Tweed Aran; medium weight #4; 55% merino wool, 25% superfine alpaca, 20% Donegal tweed; 3.5 oz. (100 g)/164 yd. (150 m) per skein
- 3 skeins: C103 Romance

Hooks and Other Materials
- US size 7 (4.5 mm) and G-6 (4 mm) crochet hooks
- Yarn needle

Finished Measurements
3–6 months: 9 in. (23 cm) chest x 9½ in. (24 cm) long
9–12 months: 9½ in. (24 cm) chest x 10 in. (25 cm) long

Gauge
Using US 7 (4.5 mm) hook, 15 sts x 12 rows = 4 in. (10 cm) in Linked Double Crochet

Special Stitches
A Linked Double Crochet row is created with a Beginning Linked Double Crochet, and then the remaining stitches will be the Linked Double Crochet.

Beginning Linked Double Crochet (Beginning Linked dc). Insert hook in second ch from hook, yarn over and pull up a loop, insert hook in st indicated, yarn over and pull up a loop (3 loops on hook), (yarn over and draw through 2 loops on hook) twice.

Linked Double Crochet (ldc). Insert hook in horizontal bar of previous link dc, yarn over and pull up a loop, insert hook in st indicated, yarn over and pull up a loop (3 loops on hook), (yarn over and draw through 2 loops on hook) twice.

Single Crochet 2 Together (sc2tog). (Insert hook, yarn over, pull up loop) in each of the sts indicated, yarn over, draw through all loops on hook.

Pattern Notes
- The sweater is made in one panel. To finish, each edge and underarm will be sewn to finish.
- See page 171 for how to work FPdc and BPdc.

INSTRUCTIONS

3–6 months

Ch 39.

Row 1 (WS): Sc in second ch from hook and in each across, turn. (38 sts)

Row 2: Ch 2, Beginning Linked dc (see Special Stitches), ldc (see Special Stitches) across, turn.

Row 3: Ch 1, sc in each st across, turn.

Row 4: Ch 2, Beginning Linked dc, ldc across, turn.

Rows 5–16: Rep Rows 3 and 4. Fasten off.

Sleeves

Row 17: Ch 20, sc in each st across, ch 21, turn.

Row 18: Using second ch Beginning Linked dc, ldc across, turn. (78 sts)

Row 19: Ch 1, sc in each st across, turn.

Row 20: Ch 2, Beginning Linked dc, ldc across, turn.

Rows 21–27: Rep Rows 19 and 20, ending on 19.

Row 28: (*Note:* Head opening is formed on this row.) Ch 2, Beginning Linked dc, ldc 26 sts, ch 24, sk 24 sts, dc in next st, ldc 26, turn.

Row 29: Ch 1, sc in each st and ch across, turn. (78 sts)

Row 30: Ch 2, Beginning Linked dc, ldc across, turn.

Rows 31–38: Rep Rows 29 and 30. Fasten off.

Row 39: Sk 20 sts, join yarn in next st, ch 1, sc in same st, sc in next 37 sts, leave remaining sts unworked, turn. (38 sts)

Row 40: Ch 2, Beginning Linked dc, ldc across, turn.

Row 41: Ch 1, sc in each st across, turn.

Rows 42–55: Rep Rows 40 and 41. Fasten off.

Fold panel in half at Rnd 28 at head opening with RS facing. Sew under arm and down body. Repeat on opposite side.

Bottom Trim

Rnd 1: Using G-6 (4 mm) hook, with RS facing, in stitch at seam, ch 2 (not a stitch), FPdc (see Special Stitches) on next st, BPdc (see Special Stitches) on next st, rep from * around, join with sl st to first FPdc.

Rnds 2–3: Ch 2, * FPdc on next FPdc, BPdc on next BPdc, rep from * around, join with sl st to first FPdc. Fasten off.

Sleeve Trim

Rnd 1: Join at seam, ch 1, use ends of rows as stitches, sc in same st as joining, sc in next 4 sts, sc2tog (see Special Stitches), * sc in next 5 sts, sc2tog, rep from * around, join with sl st to first sc.

Rnds 2–4: Ch 2, * FPdc on next FPdc, BPdc on next BPdc, rep from * around, join with sl st to first FPdc. Fasten off.

Repeat on opposite side.

9–12 months

Ch 46.

Row 1 (WS): Sc in second ch from hook and in each across, turn. (45 sts)

Row 2: Ch 2, Beginning Linked dc (see Special Stitches), ldc (see Special Stitches) across, turn.

Row 3: Ch 1, sc in each st across, turn.

Row 4: Ch 2, Beginning Linked dc, ldc across, turn.

Rows 5–20: Rep Rows 3 and 4. Fasten off.

Sleeves

Row 21: Ch 24, sc in each st across, ch 25, turn.

Row 22: Using second ch Beginning Linked dc, ldc across, turn. (93 sts)

Row 23: Ch 1, sc in each st across, turn.

Row 24: Ch 2, Beginning Linked dc, ldc across, turn.

Rows 25–33: Rep Rows 19 and 20, ending on 19.

Row 34: (*Note:* Head opening is formed on this row.) Ch 2, Beginning Linked dc, ldc 31 sts, ch 29, sk 29 sts, dc in next st, ldc 31, turn.

Row 35: Ch 1, sc in each st and ch across, turn. (93 sts)

Row 36: Ch 2, Beginning Linked dc, ldc across, turn.

Rows 37–45: Rep Rows 34 and 35. Fasten off.

Row 46: Sk 24 sts, join yarn in next st, ch 1, sc in same st, sc in next 44 sts, leave remaining sts unworked, turn. (45 sts)

Row 47: Ch 2, Beginning Linked dc, ldc across, turn.

Row 48: Ch 1, sc in each st across, turn.

Rows 49–62: Rep Rows 47 and 48. Fasten off.

Fold panel in half at Rnd 34 at head opening with RS facing. Sew under arm and down body. Repeat on opposite side.

Bottom Trim

Rnd 1: Using G-6 (4 mm) hook, with RS facing, in stitch at seam, ch 2 (not a stitch), FPdc (see Special Stitches) on next st, BPdc (see Special Stitches) on next st, rep from * around, join with sl st to first FPdc.

Rnds 2–3: Ch 2, * FPdc on next FPdc, BPdc on next BPdc, rep from * around, join with sl st to first FPdc. Fasten off.

Sleeve Trim

Rnd 1: Join at seam, ch 1, use ends of rows as stitches, sc in same st as joining, sc in next 4 sts, sc2tog (see Special Stitches), * sc in next 5 sts, sc2tog, rep from * around, join with sl st to first sc.

Rnds 2–4: Ch 2, * FPdc on next FPdc, BPdc on next BPdc, rep from * around, join with sl st to first FPdc. Fasten off.

Repeat on opposite side.

Chickie Leg Warmers

Every little crawler needs a pair of leg warmers. These are fast and easy and have the perfect stretch you need for any on-the-move baby.

Sizes
3–6 months, 9–12 months

Yarn
Lion Brand Yarns New Basic 175 Yarn; medium weight #4; 75% acrylic, 25% wool; 3.5 oz. (100 g)/175 yd. (160 m) per skein
- 1 skein: 675-106 Ice

Hook and Other Materials
- US size H-8 (5 mm) crochet hook
- Yarn needle

Finished Measurements
3–6 months: 3 in. (7.5 cm) wide x 7½ in. (19 cm) long
9–12 months: 3½ in. (9 cm) wide x 8 in. (20 cm) long

Gauge
4 sts x 4 rows = 1 in. (2.5 cm) in sc

Special Stitches
Front Post Double Crochet (FPdc). Yarn over, insert hook from front to back around post of st indicated, yarn over and pull up a loop (3 loops on hook), (yarn over and draw through 2 loops on hook) twice.

Back Post Double Crochet (BPdc). Yarn over, insert hook from back to front around post of st indicated, yarn over and pull up a loop (3 loops on hook), (yarn over and draw through 2 loops on hook) twice.

Front Post Single Crochet (FPsc). Insert hook from front to back around around post of st indicated, yarn over and pull up a loop, yarn over and draw through 2 loops on hook.

Back Post Single Crochet (BPsc). Insert hook from back to front around post of st indicated, yarn over and pull up a loop, yarn over and draw through 2 loops on hook.

INSTRUCTIONS

3–6 months

Ch 23.

Row 1: Sc in second ch from hook, dc in next ch, * sc in next ch, dc in next ch, rep from * across, turn. (22 sts)

Row 2: Ch 1, sc in blo of first st, dc in next st, * sc in blo of next st, dc in next stitch, rep from * across, turn.

Row 3: Ch 1, sc in flo of first st, dc in next st, * sc in flo of next st, dc in next st, rep from * across, turn.

Rows 4–16: Rep Row 2 and 3, ending on Row 2. Fasten off.

Use yarn needle and sew together.

Trim (top and bottom)

Rnd 1: Join yarn in stitch by seam, use ends of rows as sts, ch 2, dc in each st around, join with sl st to first dc.

Rnd 2: Ch 2, FPdc (see Special Stitches) on first dc, BPdc (see Special Stitches) on next dc, * FPdc on next dc, BPdc on next dc, rep from * around, join with sl st to first FPdc.

Rnd 3: Ch 1, FPsc (see Special Stitches) on first post, BPsc (see Special Stitches) on next post, * FPsc on next post, BPsc on next post, rep from * around, join with sl st to first FPsc.

9–12 months

Ch 27.

Row 1: Sc in second ch from hook, dc in next ch, * sc in next ch, dc in next ch, rep from * across, turn. (26 sts)

Row 2: Ch 1, sc in blo of first st, dc in next st, * sc in blo of next st, dc in next stitch, rep from * across, turn.

Row 3: Ch 1, sc in flo of first st, dc in next st, * sc in flo of next st, dc in next st, rep from * across, turn.

Rows 4–20: Rep Rows 2 and 3, ending on Row 2. Fasten off.

Use yarn needle and sew together.

Trim (top and bottom)

Rnd 1: Join yarn in stitch by seam, use ends of rows as sts, ch 2, dc in each st around, join with sl st to first dc.

Rnd 2: Ch 2, FPdc (see Special Stitches) on first dc, BPdc (see Special Stitches) on next dc, * FPdc on next dc, BPdc on next dc, rep from * around, join with sl st to first FPdc.

Rnd 3: Ch 1, FPsc (see Special Stitches) on first post, BPsc (see Special Stitches) on next post, * FPsc on next post, BPsc on next post, rep from * around, join with sl st to first FPsc.

Roly-Poly

Play Mat

Inspired by a beautiful stained-glass window, this mat works up with a unique pattern. It is the coolest mat and can also be used as a rug to add a personal touch to any room.

Yarn
Red Heart Soft Essentials; bulky weight #5; 100% acrylic; 5 oz. (141g)/131 yd. (120 m) per skein
- 2 skeins: E856-7851 Navy
- 1 skein each: E856-7305 Cream, E856-7103 Biscuit, E856-7340 Cocoa

Hook
US size K-10½ (6.5 mm) crochet hook

Finished Measurements
23 in. (58 cm) wide

Gauge
3 sts x 1 row = 1 in. (2.5 cm) in dc

Special Stitch
V-Stitch (V-st). (Dc, ch 1, dc) in same stitch.

Pattern Notes
- The beginning ch-4 counts as the first dc plus ch 1.
- The beginning ch-3 counts as the first dc.

INSTRUCTIONS

Rnd 1: With Navy, ch 4 (see Pattern Notes), 2 dc in first ch, ch 3, (3 dc in same ch, ch 3) 3 times, sl st to ch-3 of beg ch-4 to join. (12 dc, 4 ch-3 sp) Fasten off Navy.

Rnd 2: Join Cream in ch-3 sp, * ch 1, (sc, ch3, sc) in ch-3 sp, sc in next 3 dc, rep from * around, join with sl st to first sc. (20 sc, 4 ch-3 sp) Fasten off Cream.

Rnd 3: Join Navy in Rnd 1 ch-3 sp, ch 1, sc in ch-3 sp, ch-3, sc in next ch-3 sp on Rnd 1, ch 8, sc in next ch-3 sp on Rnd 1, ch 8, sc in next ch-3 sp on Rnd 1, ch 3, join with sl st in first sc. (4 ch-8 sp, 4 sc)

Rnd 4: Ch 3, 2 dc in same st, 10 dc in ch-8 sp, * dc in next sc, 10 dc in ch-8 sp, rep from * around, join with sl st to beg ch-3. (4 10-dc sets, 4 3-dc sets) Fasten off.

Rnd 5: Join Biscuit in first st, ch 3, (dc, ch 2, 2 dc) in same st, sk 3 sts, * (2 dc, ch 2, 2 dc) in next st, sk 3 sts, rep from * around, join with sl st to beg ch-3.

Rnd 6: Sl st in next st, sl st in ch-2 sp, ch 3, (2 dc, ch 2, 3 dc) in same sp, (3 dc, ch 2, 2 dc) in each ch-2 sp around, join with sl st to beg ch-3. (13 sets) Fasten off Biscuit.

Rnd 7: Join Cocoa in ch-2 sp, ch 1, sc in same st, ch 7, * sc in next ch-2 sp, ch 7, rep from * around, join with sl st to first sc. (13 ch-7, 13 sc)

Rnd 8: Ch 1, sc in same st, 8 sc in next ch-7 sp, * sc in next sc, 8 sc in next ch-7 sp, rep from * around, join with sl st to first sc. Join Cream, fasten off Cocoa. (117 sc)

Rnd 9: Ch 4, dc in same st, sk 2 sts, * V-st (see Special Stitch) in next st, sk 2 sts, rep from * around, join with sl st to ch-3 of beg ch4. (no increases; 39 sets) Fasten off.

Rnd 10: Join Navy in ch-1 sp, 2 sc in same sp, sc in next 8 sts and chs, * 2 sc in next ch-1 sp, sc in next 8 sts and chs, rep from * around, join with sl st to first sc. Join Cream, fasten off Navy

Rnd 11: Ch 1, sc in same st, sc in next 2 sts, sc in space between 2 V-sts on Rnd 9, * (sc 2, sc in space between 2 V-sts on Rnd 9) 2 times **, sc 3, sc in space between 2 V-sts on Rnd 9, rep from * around, ending last rep at **, join with sl st to first sc. Join Biscuit, fasten off Cream.

Rnd 12: Ch 1, sc in same st, * ch 4, sk 4 sts, sc in next st, rep from * around, join with sl st to first sc.

Rnd 13: Sl st to ch-4 sp, (ch 3, dc, ch 3, 2 dc) in same sp, (2 dc, ch 2, 2 dc) in each ch-4 sp, join with sl st to beg ch-3. (*Note:* Do not work in sc sts.)

Rnd 14: Sl st to ch-2 sp, ch 1, 2 sc in same sp, ch 4, * 2 sc in ch-2 sp, ch 4, rep from * around, join with sl st to first sc.

Rnd 15: Sl st to ch-4 sp, (ch 3, dc 2, ch 2, dc 3) in same sp, (dc 3, ch 2, dc 3) in each ch-4 sp, join with sl st to beg ch-3. Fasten off.

Rnd 16: Join Cocoa in ch-2 sp, ch 1, sc in same st, ch 6, * sc in next ch-2 sp, ch 6, rep from * around, join with sl st to first sc.

Rnd 17: Sl st to ch-6 sp, ch 1, 7 sc in each ch-6 sp, join with sl st to first sc. Join Cream, fasten off Cocoa.

Rnd 18: Rep Row 9. (63 sets) Fasten off.

Rnd 19: Join Navy in third st after ch-1 in V-st, * sc in next 20 sts, 2 sc in next st, rep from * around, join with sl st to first sc. Join Cream, fasten off Navy.

Rnd 20: Ch 1, sc, sc in space between 2 V-sts on Rnd 18, * (sc 2, sc in sp between 2 V-sts on Rnd 18) 6 times **, sc 3, sc in sp between 2 V-sts on Rnd 18, sc 2, rep from * around, ending last rep at **, join with sl st to first sc. Fasten off.

Rnd 21: Join Biscuit in second sc of Rnd 20, ch 1, sc in same st, ch 4, sk 4, sc in next st, ch 4, sk 4, * dc in next 2 sts, ch 4, sk 4, dc in next st **, ch 4, sk 4 rep from *, ending last rep at **, join with sl st to first sc.

Rnd 22: Sl st to ch-4 sp, (ch 3, 2 dc, ch 2, 3 dc) in same sp, (dc 3, ch 2, dc 3) in each ch-sp around, join with sl st to beg ch-3. Fasten off.

Fringe

Cut 3 strands of color at 10 in. (25.4 cm), fold in half and pull center loop through ch-2 on edge. Pull ends through center loop and tighten. Repeat around mat. Trim evenly.

Baby Burp Cloth and Bottle Cozy

This precious set is perfect for a day in town or even as a quick gift for an upcoming baby shower. Mix and match your favorite colors for the most useful gift!

Yarn

Plymouth Yarn Fantasy Naturale; medium weight #4; 100% mercerized cotton; 3.5 oz. (100 g)/140 yd. (128 m) per skein
• 1 skein each: 5228 Green (A), 9480 Blue/green variegated (B)

Hook

US size F-5 (3.75 mm) crochet hook

Finished Measurements

Burp Cloth: 9¼ in. (23 cm) wide x 9¾ in. (24 cm) long
Bottle Cozy: 4 in. (10 cm) wide x 7½ in. (19 cm) long

Gauge

4 sts x 5 rows = 1 in. (2.5 cm) in sc

Special Stitch

Single Crochet 2 Together (sc2tog). Pull up a loop in each of next 2 sc, yarn over and draw through all 3 loops on hook (counts as 1 sc).

Pattern Notes

• The beginning ch-3 counts as the first dc.
• When changing colors, complete the stitch until the last pull through; drop working yarn, pull through next color as last pull through to complete color change and finish stitch.

INSTRUCTIONS

Burp Cloth

With Color A, ch 34.

Row 1: Dc in 4th ch from hook and in each across, turn. Join Color B, fasten off Color A (see Pattern Notes). (32 sts)

Row 2: Ch 3 (see Pattern Notes), * dc in next st, dc on the previous dc post just made, sk 1 st, rep from * across, dc in last st, turn. Join Color A, fasten off Color B.

Row 3: Ch 3, dc in each st across, turn. Join Color B, fasten off Color A.

Row 4: Rep Row 2.

Rows 5–17: Ch 3, dc in each st across, turn. Join Color B, fasten off Color A.

Row 18: Rep Row 2.

Row 19: Ch 3, dc in each st across, turn. Join Color B, fasten off Color A.

Row 20: Rep Row 2.

Row 21: Ch 3, dc in each st across, turn. Fasten off.

Bottle Cozy

With Color A, ch 2.

Rnd 1: 6 sc in second ch from hook, join with sl st to first sc. (6 sc)

Rnd 2: Ch 1, 2 sc in each st around, join with sl st to first sc. (12 sts)

Rnd 3: Ch 1, sc in same st, 2 sc in next st, * sc in next st, 2 sc in next st, rep from * around, join with sl st to first sc. (18 sts)

Rnd 4: Ch 1, sc in same st, sc in next st, 2 sc in next st, *sc in next 2 sts, 2 sc in next st, rep from * around, join with sl st to first sc. (24 sts)

Rnd 5: Ch 1, sc in same st, sc in next 2 sts, 2 sc in next st, * sc in next 3 sts, 2 sc in next st, rep from * around, join with sl st to first sc. (30 sts)

Rnd 6: Ch 1, working in the back loop only, sc in each st around, join with sl st to first sc.

Rnd 7: Ch 1, sc in each st around, join with sl st to first sc. Join Color B, fasten off Color A.

Rnd 8: Ch 3 (see Pattern Notes), dc in ch-3 just made, sk 1 st, * dc in next st, dc in the previous dc post just made, sk 1 st, rep from * around, join with sl st to beg ch-3.

Rnd 9: Ch 1, sc in each st around, join with sl st to first sc.

Rnds 10–16: Rep Rnds 8 and 9, ending on Rnd 8. Join Color A, fasten off Color B.

Rnds 17–18: Ch 1, sc in each st around, join with sl st to first sc.

Rnd 19: Ch 1, sc in same st, sc in next 2 sts, sc2tog (see Special Stitch), * sc in next 3 sts, sc2tog, rep from * around, join with sl st to first sc. Fasten off.

Hopscotch Baby Booties

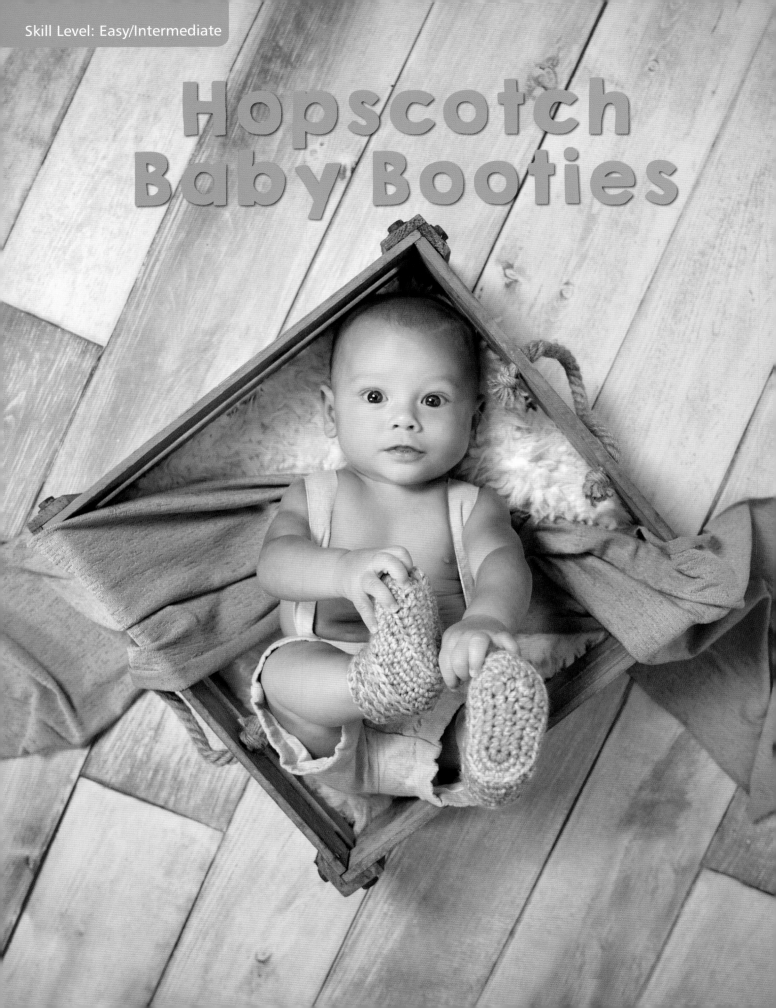

Babies will be stepping (or scooting) in style in these sweet booties! These are customizable for boys or girls simply by changing the colors.

Sizes
Small, Medium

Yarn
Red Heart Hopscotch; medium weight #4; 100% acrylic; 4 oz. (113 g)/210 yd. (193 m) per skein
- 1 skein: E860-7950 Scooter

Hook
US size F-5 (3.75 mm) crochet hook

Finished Measurements
Small: 2 in. (5 cm) wide x 3 in. (7.5 cm) long
Medium: 2 in. (5 cm) wide x 3½ in. (9 cm) long

Gauge
5 sts x 5 rows = 1 in. (2.5 cm) in sc

Special Stitches
Single Crochet 2 Together (sc2tog). (Insert hook, yarn over, pull up loop) in each of the sts indicated, yarn over, draw through all loops on hook.
Half Double Crochet 2 Together (hdc2tog). Yarn over, pull up a loop in st, yarn over, pull up a loop in next st, yarn over, pull through all loops on hook (counts as 1 hdc).
Double Crochet 2 Together (dc2tog). Yarn over, pull up a loop in next st, yarn over, pull through first 2 loops, yarn over, pull up a loop in the next stitch, yarn over and draw through first 2 loops, yarn over, pull through all loops on hook (counts as 1 dc).

Pattern Notes
- The booties are made from sole to cuff.
- The beginning ch-2 will not count as a stitch unless otherwise indicated.

INSTRUCTIONS

Small

Ch 8.

Rnd 1: Sc in second ch from hook and in each ch across to last ch, 4 hdc in last ch, working in free loops of beginning ch, sc in next 5 chs, 3 sc in next ch, join with sl st to first sc. (18 sts)

Rnd 2: Ch1, sc in same st as joining and in next 3 sts, hdc in next 2 sts, 2 dc in each of next 4 sts, hdc in next 2 sts, sc in next 3 sts, 2 sc in each of last 3 sts, join with sl st to first st. (25 sts)

Rnd 3: Ch 2 (see Pattern Notes), hdc in same st as joining and in next 6 sts, 2 hdc in next st, (hdc in next st, 2 hdc in next st) 3 times, hdc in next 5 sts, (sc in next sc, 2 sc in next st) 3 times, join with sl st to first st. (32 sts)

Rnd 4: Ch 1, working in back loop only, sc in each st around, join with sl st to the first sc.

Rnd 5: Ch 1, sc in each st around, join with sl st to the first sc.

Rnd 6: Ch 1, sc in same st as joining and in next 3 sts, sc2tog (see Special Stitches), hdc2tog (see Special Stitches), dc2tog (see Special Stitches) 4 times, hdc2tog, sc2tog, sc in each st to end, join with sl st to first sc. (24 sts)

Rnd 7: Ch 1, sc in same st as joining and in next 3 sts, hdc2tog, dc2tog 2 times, sc in each st to end, join with sl st to first sc. (21 sts)

Rnd 8: Ch 2, hdc in each st around, join with sl st to first hdc.

Rnds 9–12: Ch 2, hdc in each of the back horizontal bar in previous rnd hdc around, join with sl st to first hdc. Fasten off.

Medium

Ch 10.

Rnd 1: Sc in second ch from hook and in each ch across to last ch, 4 hdc in last ch, working in free loops of beginning ch, sc in next 7 chs, 3 sc in next ch, join with sl st to first sc. (22 sts)

Rnd 2: Ch1, sc in same st as joining and in next 5 sts, hdc in next 2 sts, 2 dc in each of next 4 sts, hdc in next 2 sts, sc in next 5 sts, 2 sc in each of last 3 sts, join with sl st to first st. (29 sts)

Rnd 3: Ch 2 (see Pattern Notes), hdc in same st as joining and in next 8 sts, 2 hdc in next st, (hdc in next st, 2 hdc in next st) 3 times, hdc in next 5 sts, (sc in next sc, 2 sc in next st) 3 times, join with sl st to first st. (36 sts)

Rnd 4: Ch 1, working in back loop only, sc in each st around, join with sl st to the first sc.

Rnd 5: Ch 1, sc in each st around, join with sl st to the first sc.

Rnd 6: Ch 1, sc in same st as joining and in next 5 sts, sc2tog (see Special Stitches), hdc2tog (see Special Stitches), dc2tog (see Special Stitches) 4 times, hdc2tog, sc2tog, sc in each st to end, join with sl st to first sc. (28 sts)

Rnd 7: Ch 1, sc in same st as joining and in next 3 sts, hdc2tog, dc2tog 2 times, sc in each st to end, join with sl st to first sc. (25 sts)

Rnd 8: Ch 2, hdc in each st around, join with sl st to first hdc.

Rnds 9–12: Ch 2, hdc in each of the back horizontal bar in previous rnd hdc around, join with sl st to first hdc. Fasten off.

Doodlebug Capris

These capris are as cute as a button! They are made from the top down and finished with a fun ruffle. A must-have for any little girl.

Sizes
3–6 months, 6–9 months, 9–12 months

Yarn
Plymouth Yarn Encore Worsted; medium weight #4; 75% acrylic, 25% wool; 3.5 oz. (100 g)/200 yd. (183 m) per skein
- 1 skein each: 449 Pink, 1201 Pale Green, 208 White

Hook and Other Materials
- US size H-8 (5 mm) crochet hook
- Yarn needle

Finished Measurements
3–6 months: 15 in. (38 cm) waist x 10 in. (25 cm) long
6–9 months: 16½ in. (42 cm) waist x 11 in. (28 cm) long
9–12 months: 17½ in. (44 cm) waist x 11½ in. (29 cm) long

Gauge
15 sts x 6 rows = 4 in. (10 cm) in dc

Special Stitches
Front Post Double Crochet (FPdc). Yarn over, insert hook from front to back around post of st indicated, yarn over and pull up a loop (3 loops on hook), (yarn over and draw through 2 loops on hook) twice.
Back Post Double Crochet (BPdc). Yarn over, insert hook from back to front around post of st indicated, yarn over and pull up a loop (3 loops on hook), (yarn over and draw through 2 loops on hook) twice.

Pattern Note
- The beginning ch-2 will not count as a stitch. It is used to help create a seamless join.

INSTRUCTIONS

3–6 months

With Pale Green, ch 55.

Rnd 1: Sc in second ch from hook and in each ch around, join with sl st to first sc. (54 sts)

Rnd 2: Ch 2 (see Pattern Note), FPdc (see Special Stitches) on first st, BPdc (see Special Stitches) on next st, * FPdc on next st, BPdc on next st, rep from * around, join with sl st to first FPdc.

Rnds 3–5: Ch 2, * FPdc on next FPdc post below, BPdc on next BPdc post below, rep from * around, join with sl st to first FPdc. Join White, fasten off Pale Green.

Rnd 6: Ch 1, sc in each st, join with sl st to first sc.

Rnd 7: Ch 2, dc in joining st, dc in each st around, join with sl st to first dc. Join Pale Green, fasten off White.

Rnds 8–9: Rep Rnds 6–7. Join White, fasten off Pale Green.

Rnds 10–15: Rep Rnds 6–9 ending with Rnd 7. Join Pale Green, fasten off White.

Leg 1

Rnd 16: With Pale Green, ch 1, sc 31, join with sl st to first sc. (27 sts)

Rnd 17: Ch 2, dc in joining st, dc in each st around, join with sl st to first dc. Join White, fasten off Pale Green.

Rnd 18: Ch 1, sc in each st, join with sl st to first sc.

Rnd 19: Ch 2, dc in joining st, dc in each st around, join with sl st to first dc. Join Pale Green, fasten off White.

Rnds 20–23: Rep Rnds 18–21. Join Pink, fasten off White.

Rnd 24: Ch 3, 3 dc in joining st, 4 dc in each st around, join with sl st to beg ch-3. Fasten off.

Leg 2

Rnd 16: With Pale Green, join in next worked st, ch 1, sc 31, join with sl st to first sc. (27 sts)

Rnd 17: Ch 2, dc in joining st, dc in each st around, join with sl st to first dc. Join White, fasten off Pale Green.

Rnd 18: Ch 1, sc in each st, join with sl st to first sc.

Rnd 19: Ch 2, dc in joining st, dc in each st around, join with sl st to first dc. Join Pale Green, fasten off White.

Rnds 20–23: Rep Rnds 18–21. Join Pink, fasten off White.

Rnd 24: Ch 3, 3 dc in joining st, 4 dc in each st around, join with sl st to beg ch-3. Fasten off.

Tie

With Pink, ch 90. Fasten off.

Starting in the front middle, use FPdc on Rnd 2 to weave around waist. Tie in front.

6–9 months

With Pale Green, ch 59.

Rnd 1: Sc in second ch from hook and in each ch around, join with sl st to first sc. (58 sts)

Rnd 2: Ch 2 (see Pattern Note), FPdc (see Special Stitches) on first st, BPdc (see Special Stitches) on next st, * FPdc on next st, BPdc on next st, rep from * around, join with sl st to first FPdc.

Rnds 3–5: Ch 2, * FPdc on next FPdc post below, BPdc on next BPdc post below, rep from * around, join with sl st to first FPdc. Join White, fasten off Pale Green.

Rnd 6: Ch 1, sc in each st, join with sl st to first sc.

Rnd 7: Ch 2, dc in joining st, dc in each st around, join with sl st to first dc. Join Pale Green, fasten off White.

Rnds 8–9: Rep Rnds 6–7. Join White, fasten off Pale Green.

Rnds 10–15: Rep Rnds 6–9, ending with Rnd 7. Join Pale Green, fasten off White.

Leg 1

Rnd 16: With Pale Green, ch 1, sc 31, join with sl st to first sc. (29 sts)

Rnd 17: Ch 2, dc in joining st, dc in each st around, join with sl st to first dc. Join White, fasten off Pale Green.

Rnd 18: Ch 1, sc in each st, join with sl st to first sc.

Rnd 19: Ch 2, dc in joining st, dc in each st around, join with sl st to first dc. Join Pale Green, fasten off White.

Rnds 20–25: Rep Rnds 18–21. Join Pink, fasten off White.

Rnd 26: Ch 3, 3 dc in joining st, 4 dc in each st around, join with sl st to beg ch-3. Fasten off.

Leg 2

Rnd 16: With Pale Green, join in next worked st, ch 1, sc 31, join with sl st to first sc. (29 sts)

Rnd 17: Ch 2, dc in joining st, dc in each st around, join with sl st to first dc. Join White, fasten off Pale Green.

Rnd 18: Ch 1, sc in each st, join with sl st to first sc.

Rnd 19: Ch 2, dc in joining st, dc in each st around, join with sl st to first dc. Join Pale Green, fasten off White.

Rnds 20–25: Rep Rnds 18–21. Join Pink, fasten off White.

Rnd 26: Ch 3, 3 dc in joining st, 4 dc in each st around, join with sl st to beg ch-3. Fasten off.

Tie

With Pink, ch 100. Fasten off.

Starting in the front middle, use FPdc on Rnd 2 to weave around waist. Tie in front.

9–12 months

With Pale Green, ch 63.

Rnd 1: Sc in second ch from hook and in each ch around, join with sl st to first sc. (62 sts)

Rnd 2: Ch 2 (see Pattern Note), FPdc (see Special Stitches) on first st, BPdc (see Special Stitches) on next st, * FPdc on next st, BPdc on next st, rep from * around, join with sl st to first FPdc.

Rnds 3–5: Ch 2, * FPdc on next Fpdc post below, BPdc on next BPdc post below, rep from * around, join with sl st to first FPdc. Join White, fasten off Pale Green.

Rnd 6: Ch 1, sc in each st, join with sl st to first sc.

Rnd 7: Ch 2, dc in joining st, dc in each st around, join with sl st to first dc. Join Pale Green, fasten off White.

Rnds 8–9: Rep Rnds 6–7. Join White, fasten off Pale Green.

Rnds 10–17: Rep Rnds 6–9 twice.

Leg 1

Rnd 18: With White, ch 1, sc 31, join with sl st to first sc. (31 sts)

Rnd 19: Ch 2, dc in joining st, dc in each st around, join with sl st to first dc. Join Pale Green, fasten off White.

Rnd 20: Ch 1, sc in each st, join with sl st to first sc.

Rnd 21: Ch 2, dc in joining st, dc in each st around, join with sl st to first dc. Join White, fasten off Pale Green.

Rnds 22–29: Rep Rnds 18–21. Join Pink, fasten off Pale Green.

Rnd 30: Ch 3, 3 dc in joining st, 4 dc in each st around, join with sl st to beg ch-3. Fasten off.

Leg 2

Rnd 18: With White, join in next worked st, ch 1, sc 31, join with sl st to first sc. (31 sts)

Rnd 19: Ch 2, dc in joining st, dc in each st around, join with sl st to first dc. Join Pale Green, fasten off White.

Rnd 20: Ch 1, sc in each st, join with sl st to first sc.

Rnd 21: Ch 2, dc in joining st, dc in each st around, join with sl st to first dc. Join White, fasten off Pale Green.

Rnds 22–29: Rep Rnds 18–21. Join Pink, fasten off Pale Green.

Rnd 30: Ch 3, 3 dc in joining st, 4 dc in each st around, join with sl st to beg ch-3. Fasten off.

Tie

With Pink, ch 100. Fasten off.

Starting in the front middle, use FPdc on Rnd 2 to weave around waist. Tie in front.

Giggles the Owl Pillow

This sweet and sassy owl will be a hit with anyone on your gifting list. The feather stitching is fun and adds the perfect texture.

Yarn

Red Heart Chic Sheep; medium weight #4; 100% wool; 3.5 oz. (100 g)/186 yd. (170 m) per skein

- 1 skein each: R170-5635 Creme de Mint (A), R170-5673 Fairy Tale (B), R170-5324 Mimosa (C), R170-5311 Lace (D), R170-5312 Stiletto (E)

Hook and Other Materials

- US size F-5 (3.75 mm) crochet hook
- Yarn needle
- Stitch markers

Finished Measurement

7 in. (18 cm) wide x 8½ in. (22 cm) long

Gauge

16 sts x 16 rows = 4 in. (10 cm) in sc

Special Stitches

Crocodile Stitch. 5 dc down the first dc post, ch 1, 5 dc up the next dc post.

Single Crochet 2 Together (sc2tog). Pull up a loop in each of next 2 sc, yarn over and draw through all 3 loops on hook (counts as 1 sc).

Pattern Notes

- The front panel is made from bottom to top.
- The back panel is made from top to bottom.
- The beginning ch-2 will not count as a stitch. It is used to help create a seamless join.

INSTRUCTIONS

Front Panel

With Color A, ch 26.

Row 1: Sc in second ch from hook and in each ch across, turn. (25 sts)

Row 2: Ch 3, dc in same st, * sk 1 st, 2 dc in next st, rep from * across. (26 sts)

Row 3: Ch 3, 4 dc on first post, ch 1, turn, 4 dc up next post (first Crocodile Stitch complete; see Special Stitches), * sk 2 dc, Crocodile Stitch over next 2 dc, rep from * across, turn. (7 Crocodile Stitches) Fasten off.

Row 4: Insert Color B in edge of last Crocodile Stitch, ch 3, dc in same st, 2 dc in center of next Crocodile Stitch, * 2 dc between next 2 dc sets and over ends of Crocodile Stitch, 2 dc in center of next Crocodile Stitch, rep from * across, ending with 2 dc in edge of last Crocodile Stitch. (30 sts)

Row 5: Rep Row 3. (8 Crocodile Stitches)

Row 6: Insert Color C in center of last Crocodile Stitch, ch 3, dc in same st, * 2 dc between next 2 dc sets and over ends of Crocodile Stitch, 2 dc in center of next Crocodile Stitch, rep from * across, turn.

Row 7: Skip first 2 dc, Crocodile Stitch on next 2 dc, * sk 2 dc, Crocodile Stitch on next 2 dc, rep from * across, sk 1 dc, sl st in top of last dc, turn. Fasten off. (7 Crocodile Stitches)

Row 8: Using Color A, rep Row 4.

Row 9: Rep Row 3.

Row 10: Using Color B, rep Row 6.

Row 11: Rep Row 7.

Row 12: Using Color C, rep Row 4.

Row 13: Rep Row 3.

Row 14: Using Color A, rep Row 6.

Row 15: Rep Row 7, do not fasten off Color A.

Row 16: Ch 1, 2 sc in end of Crocodile Stitch, 2 sc in center of Crocodile Stitch, * 2 sc between next 2 dc and over ends of Crocodile Stitch, 2 sc in center of Crocodile Stitch, rep from * across, ending with 2 sc in end of Crocodile Stitch, turn. (30 sts)

Rows 17–19: Ch 1, sc in each st across, turn.

Row 20: Sc2tog (see Special Stitches), sc to last 2 sts, sc2tog, turn. (28 sts)

Rows 21–27: Ch 1, sc in each st across, turn.

Row 28: Sc2tog, sc to last 2 sts, sc2tog. (26 sts)

Rows 29–31: Ch 1, sc in each st across, turn.

Row 32: Sc2tog, sc to last 2 sts, sc2tog. (24 sts)

Rows 33–34: Ch 1, sc in each st across, turn.

Row 35: Sc2tog, sc to last 2 sts, sc2tog, turn. (22 sts)

Row 36: Sc2tog, sc to last 2 sts, sc2tog, turn. (20 sts)

Row 37: Sc2tog, sc to last 2 sts, sc2tog, turn. (18 sts)

Row 38: Sc2tog, sc to last 2 sts, sc2tog, turn. (16 sts)

Row 39: Sc2tog, sc to last 2 sts, sc2tog, turn. (14 sts) Fasten off.

Trim

Sc evenly around using ends of rows as stitches. Work in the back inside post of the dc in the Crocodile Stitches so that they are free on the ends when sewn together with Back Panel.

Back Panel

With Color A, ch 15.

Row 1: Sc in second ch from hook and in each ch across, turn. (14 sts)

Row 2: Ch 1, 2 sc in first st, sc 12, 2 sc in last st, turn. (16 sts)

Row 3: Ch 1, 2 sc in first st, sc 14, 2 sc in last st, turn. (18 sts)

Row 4: Ch 1, 2 sc in first st, sc 16, 2 sc in last st, turn. (20 sts)

Row 5: Ch 1, 2 sc in first st, sc 18, 2 sc in last st, turn. (22 sts)

Rows 6–7: Ch 1, sc in each st across, turn.

Row 8: Ch 1, 2 sc in first st, sc 20, 2 sc in last st, turn. (24 sts)

Rows 9–11: Ch 1, sc in each st across, turn.

Row 12: Ch 1, 2 sc in first st, sc 22, 2 sc in last st, turn. (26 sts)

Rows 13–19: Ch 1, sc in each st across, turn.

Row 20: Ch 1, 2 sc in first st, sc 24, 2 sc in last st, turn. (28 sts)

Rows 21–23: Ch 1, sc in each st across, turn.

Row 24: Ch 1, 2 sc in first st, sc 26, 2 sc in last st, turn. (30 sts)

Rows 25–36: Ch 1, sc in each st across, turn.

Row 37: Sc2tog, sc 26, sc2tog, turn. (28 sts)

Row 38: Ch 1, sc in each st across, fasten off.

Trim

Sc evenly around, using ends of rows as stitches.

Eyes
Back
With Lace, ch 4.

Rnd 1: 10 dc in first ch, join with sl st to first dc. (10 dc)

Rnd 2: Ch 2 (see Pattern Notes), 2 dc in each st, join with sl st to first dc. (20 sts)

Rnd 3: Ch 1, sc in first st, 2 sc in next st, * sc in next st, 2 sc in next, rep from * around, join with sl st to first sc. (30 sts) Fasten off, leaving long end for sewing.

Pupil
With Stiletto, ch 2.

Rnd 1: 6 sc in second ch from hook, join with sl st to first st. Fasten off, leaving long end for sewing.

Assembly
Using yarn needle, sew Pupil onto Back of Eye, and then sew completed Eye onto Front Panel.

Place WS of Body panels together and sew together, stuffing firmly before closing.

Nose
Using yarn needle, stitch on nose.

Finishing
Cut two pieces of yarn 4 in. (10 cm) in each color.

Take one piece of each color; fold in half and pull center loop through top corners. Pull ends through loop and tighten. Trim evenly.

Bubba Baby Vest

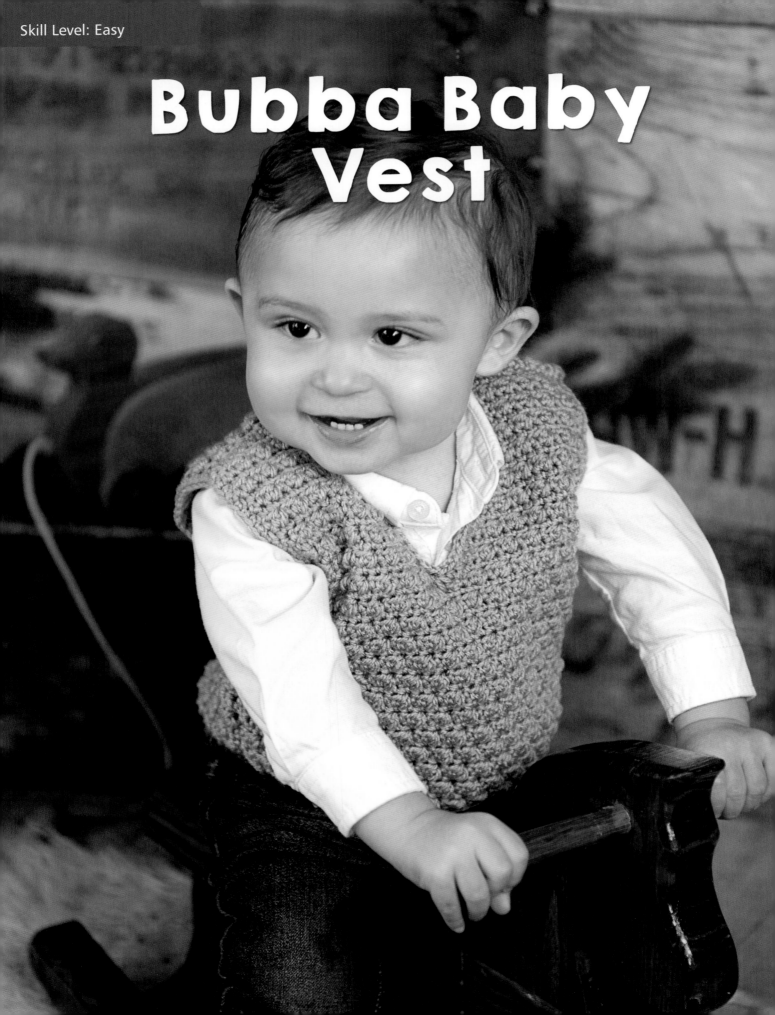

This classic V-neck vest is the perfect accessory for anyone who loves a fashionable baby. It's made with single crochet and clusters to add the perfect texture to a simple design.

Sizes
3–6 months, 9–12 months

Yarn
Red Heart Hugs; medium weight #4; 100% acrylic; 4.5 oz. (127 g)/318 yd. (290 m) per skein
- 2 skeins: E403-3410 Dolphin

Hooks and Other Materials
- US size 7 (4.5 mm) and G-6 (4 mm) crochet hooks
- Yarn needle

Finished Measurement
3–6 months: 10 in. (25 cm) chest x 9½ in. (24 cm) long
9–12 months: 11 in. (28 cm) chest x 10 in. (25 cm) long

Gauge
With 7 (4.5 mm) crochet hook, 16 sts x 16 rows = 4 in. (10 cm) in sc

Special Stitches
Cluster (cl). Holding back last loop of each stitch on hook, 2 dc in stitch indicated, yarn over, pull through all loops on hook.

Single Crochet 2 Together (sc2tog). (Insert hook, yarn over, pull up loop) in each of the sts indicated, yarn over, draw through all loops on hook.

Half Double Crochet 3 Together (hdc3tog). Yarn over, pull up a loop in st, (yarn over, pull up a loop in next st) 2 times, yarn over, pull through all loops on hook (counts as 1 hdc).

Pattern Note
- The Vest is made in 2 parts: Back and Front. The front will be made and then split to right and left side to create a V-Neck.

INSTRUCTIONS
3–6 months

Back

With US 7 (4.5 mm) hook, ch 38.

Row 1 (RS): Sc in second ch from hook and in each across, turn. (37 sts)

Row 2: Ch 1, sc in first st, * cl (see Special Stitches) in next st, sc in next st, rep from * across, turn.

Row 3: Ch 1, sc in each st across, turn.

Row 4: Ch 1, sc in first st, sc in next st, cl in next st, * sc in next st, cl in next st, rep from * across, sc in last 2 sc, turn.

Row 5: Rep Row 3.

Rows 6–18: Rep Rows 2–5, ending on Row 2.

Row 19: Sc2tog (see Special Stitches) 2 times, sc to last 4 sts, sc2tog 2 times, turn. (33 sts)

Row 20: Rep Row 4.
Row 21: Sc2tog, sc to last 2 sts, sc2tog. (31 sts)
Row 22: Rep Row 4.
Row 23: Sc2tog, sc to last 2 sts, sc2tog. (29 sts)
Row 24: Rep Row 4.
Row 25: Ch 1, sc in each st across, turn.
Rows 26–37: Rep Rows 2–5 three times. Fasten off.

Front

Rep Rows 1–23 of Back Panel.

Left Side

Row 24: Ch 1, sc in the first st, sc in next st, [cl in next st, sc in next st] 7 times, sc in next st, turn.
Row 25: Sc2tog, sc to last 2 sts, sc2tog, turn.
Row 26: Ch 1, sc in the first st, sc in next st, cl in next st, * sc in next st, cl in next st, rep from * across to last 2 sts, sc in last 2 sts, turn.
Row 27: Rep Row 25.
Row 28: Rep Row 26.
Row 29: Sc2tog, sc to last st, turn.
Row 30: Ch 1, sc in first st, cl in next st, * sc in next st, cl in next st, rep from * across to last 2 sts, sc in last 2 sts, turn.
Row 31: Rep Row 29.
Row 32: Ch 1, sc in first st, sc in next st, cl in next st, * sc in next st, cl in next st, rep from * across to last 2 sts, sc in last 2 sts, turn.
Row 33: Rep Row 29.
Row 34: Rep Row 30.
Row 35: Ch 1, sc in each st across, turn.
Row 36: Ch 1, sc in first st, sc in next st, * cl in next st, sc in next st, rep from * across, turn.
Row 37: Ch 1, sc in each st across. Fasten off.

Right Side

Rep Rows 1–23 of Back Panel.

Row 24: Ch 1, sc in same st, * sc in next st, cl in next st, rep from * across to last 2 sts, sc in last 2 sts, turn.
Row 25: Sc2tog, sc to last 2 sts, sc2tog, turn.
Row 26: Ch 1, sc in first st, sc in next st, cl in next st, * sc in next st, cl in next st, rep from * across to last 2 sts, turn.
Row 27: Rep Row 25.
Row 28: Rep Row 26.
Row 29: Ch 1, sc in each st across to last 2 sts, sc2tog, turn.
Row 30: Ch 1, sc in first st, sc in next st, * cl in next st, sc in next st, rep from * across, turn.
Row 31: Rep Row 29.
Row 32: Ch 1, sc in first st, sc in next st, cl in next st, * sc in next st, cl in next st, rep from * across to last 2 sts, sc in last 2 sts, turn.

Row 33: Rep Row 29.
Row 34: Rep Row 30.
Row 35: Ch 1, sc in each st across, turn.
Row 36: Ch 1, sc in first st, * cl in next st, sc in next st, rep from * across, sc in last st, turn.
Row 37: Ch 1, sc in each st across. Fasten off.

9–12 months

Back

With US 7 (4.5 mm) hook, ch 42.

Row 1 (RS): Sc in second ch from hook and in each across, turn. (41 sts)
Row 2: Ch 1, sc in first st, * cl (see Special Stitches) in next st, sc in next st, rep from * across, turn.
Row 3: Ch 1, sc in each st across, turn.
Row 4: Ch 1, sc in first st, sc in next st, cl in next st, * sc in next st, cl in next st, rep from * across, sc in last 2 sc, turn.
Row 5: Rep Row 3.
Rows 6–22: Rep Rows 2–5, ending on Row 2.
Row 23: Sc2tog (see Special Stitches) 2 times, sc to last 4 sts, sc2tog 2 times, turn. (37 sts)
Row 24: Rep Row 4.
Row 25: Sc2tog, sc to last 2 sts, sc2tog. (35 sts)
Row 26: Rep Row 4.
Row 27: Sc2tog, sc to last 2 sts, sc2tog. (33 sts)
Row 28: Rep Row 4.
Row 29: Ch 1, sc in each st across, turn.
Rows 30–41: Rep Rows 2–5 three times. Fasten off.

Front

Rep Rows 1–23 of Back Panel.

Left Side

Row 24: Ch 1, sc in the first st, sc in next st, [cl in next st, sc in next st] 8 times, sc in next st, turn.
Row 25: Sc2tog, sc to last 2 sts, sc2tog, turn.
Row 26: Ch 1, sc in the first st, sc in next st, cl in next st, * sc in next st, cl in next st, rep from * across to last 2 sts, sc in last 2 sts, turn.
Row 27: Rep Row 25.
Row 28: Rep Row 26.
Row 29: Sc2tog, sc to last st, turn.
Row 30: Ch 1, sc in first st, cl in next st, * sc in next st, cl in next st, rep from * across to last 2 sts, sc in last 2 sts, turn.
Row 31: Rep Row 29.
Row 32: Ch 1, sc in first st, sc in next st, cl in next st, * sc in next st, cl in next st, rep from * across to last 2 sts, sc in last 2 sts, turn.
Row 33: Rep Row 29.
Row 34: Rep Row 30.
Row 35: Rep Row 29.

Row 36: Rep Row 32.
Row 37: Rep Row 29.
Row 38: Rep Row 30.
Row 39: Ch 1, sc in each st across, turn.
Row 40: Ch 1, sc in first st, sc in next st, * cl in next st, sc in next st, rep from * across, turn.
Row 41: Ch 1, sc in each st across. Fasten off.

Right Side
Row 24: Ch 1, sc in same st, * sc in next st, cl in next st, rep from * across to last 2 sts, sc in last 2 sts, turn.
Row 25: Sc2tog, sc to last 2 sts, sc2tog, turn.
Row 26: Ch 1, sc in first st, sc in next st, cl in next st, * sc in next st, cl in next st, rep from * across to last 2 sts, turn.
Row 27: Rep Row 25.
Row 28: Rep Row 26.
Row 29: Ch 1, sc in each st across to last 2 sts, sc2tog, turn.
Row 30: Ch 1, sc in first st, sc in next st, * cl in next st, sc in next st, rep from * across, turn.
Row 31: Rep Row 29.
Row 32: Ch 1, sc in first st, sc in next st, cl in next st, * sc in next st, cl in next st, rep from * across to last 2 sts, sc in last 2 sts, turn.
Row 33: Rep Row 29.
Row 34: Rep Row 30.
Row 35: Rep Row 29.
Row 36: Rep Row 32.
Row 37: Rep Row 30.

Row 38: Rep Row 29.
Row 39: Ch 1, sc in each st across, turn.
Row 40: Ch 1, sc in first st, * cl in next st, sc in next st, rep from * across, sc in last st, turn.
Row 41: Ch 1, sc in each st across. Fasten off.

Both sizes
Assembly
With right sides together, sew shoulder seams and side seams together.

Trim
Armholes
Using a G-6 (4 mm) crochet hook, join at seam, ch 1, sc evenly across ends of rows, join with sl st to first sc. Fasten off.

Neck
Using a G-6 (4 mm) crochet hook, join at shoulder seam, ch 1, sc across Back Panel, hdc evenly across ends of rows to point, hdc3tog (see Special Stitches) using the last stitch of row, the center stitch of point, and next st of next side, hdc evenly across ends of rows to first sc, join with sl st to first sc. Fasten off.

Bottom
Using a G-6 (4 mm) crochet hook, join at seam, ch 2, hdc in each st around, join with sl st to first hdc. Fasten off.

Button Up Sweater

Adorable and fun, this sweater is made with a medium-weight yarn and basic stitches. Don't be intimidated by seaming; it's easy! Give this pattern a try, and you'll be hooked with this classic sweater.

Sizes
3–6 months, 9–12 months

Yarn
Patons Yarn Decor; medium weight #4; 75% acrylic, 25% wool; 3.5 oz. (100 g)/208 yd. (190 m) per skein
- 1 skein: 87672 Gray Heather (A)
- 2 skeins: 87692 Sweet Country Variegated (B)

Hook and Other Materials
- US size F-5 (3.75 mm) crochet hook
- Yarn needle
- Stitch markers
- 6 buttons (1 in./2.5 cm)
- Sewing needle and matching thread

Finished Measurements
3–6 months: 10 in. (25 cm) chest x 8 in. (20 cm) long
9–12 months: 11 in. (28 cm) chest x 8½ in. (22 cm) long

Gauge
16 sts x 18 rows = 4 in. (10 cm) in sc

Special Stitch
Single Crochet 2 Together (sc2tog). Pull up a loop in each of next 2 sc, yarn over, and draw through all 3 loops on hook (counts as 1 sc).

Pattern Note
- The sweater is crocheted in separate sections and then sewn together.

INSTRUCTIONS
3–6 months
Front Left
With Color A, ch 19.
Row 1 (RS): Sc in second ch from hook and in each ch across, turn. (18 sts)
Rows 2–4: Ch 1, sc in each st across, turn. Fasten off.

Rows 5–20: Join Color B, ch 1, sc in each st across, turn.
Row 21: Ch 1, sc in each st to last st, 2 sc in last st. (19 sts)
Row 22: Ch 1, 2sc in first st, sc in each st across, turn. (20 sts)
Row 23: Ch 1, sc in each st to last 2 sts, sc2tog (see Special Stitch), turn. (19 sts)

Row 24: Sc2tog, sc in each st across, turn. (18 sts)

Row 25: Ch 1, sc in each st to last 2 sts, sc2tog, turn. (17 sts)

Row 26: Sc2tog, sc in each st across, turn. (16 sts)

Row 27: Ch 1, sc in each st to last 2 sts, sc2tog, turn. (15 sts)

Row 28: Sc2tog, sc in each st across, turn. (14 sts)

Rows 29–34: Ch 1, sc in each st across, turn.

Row 35: Sc2tog, sc in each st across, turn. (13 sts)

Row 36: Ch 1, sc in each st to last 2 sts, sc2tog, turn. (12 sts)

Row 37: Sc2tog, sc in each st across, turn. (11 sts)

Row 38: Ch 1, sc in each st across to last 4 sts, sc2tog 2 times, turn. (9 sts)

Row 39: Sc2tog, sc in each st across, turn. (8 sts)

Row 40: Ch 1, sc in each st across to last 4 sts, sc2tog 2 times, turn. (6 sts)

Row 41: Sc2tog, sc in each st across, turn. (5 sts)

Rows 42–43: Ch 1, sc in each st across. Fasten off.

Front Right

With Color A, ch 19.

Row 1 (RS): Sc in second ch from hook and in each ch across, turn. (18 sts)

Rows 2–4: Ch 1, sc in each st across, turn. Fasten off.

Rows 5–20: Join Color B, ch 1, sc in each st across, turn.

Row 21: Ch 1, 2 sc in first st, sc in each st across, turn. (19 sts)

Row 22: Ch 1, sc in each st to last st, 2 sc in last st, turn. (20 sts)

Row 23: Sc2tog, sc in each st across, turn. (19 sts)

Row 24: Ch 1, sc in each st to last 2 sts, sc2tog, turn. (18 sts)

Row 25: Sc2tog, sc in each st across, turn. (17 sts)

Row 26: Ch 1, sc in each st to last 2 sts, sc2tog, turn. (16 sts)

Row 27: Sc2tog, sc in each st across, turn. (15 sts)

Row 28: Ch 1, sc in each st to last 2 sts, sc2tog, turn. (14 sts)

Rows 29–34: Ch 1, sc in each st across, turn.

Row 35: Ch 1, sc in each st across to last 2 sts, sc2tog, turn. (13 sts)

Row 36: Sc2tog, sc in each st across, turn. (12 sts)

Row 37: Ch 1, sc in each st across to last 2 sts, sc2tog, turn. (11 sts)

Row 38: Sc2tog 2 times, sc in each st across, turn. (9 sts)

Row 39: Ch 1, sc in each st across to last 2 sts, sc2tog, turn. (8 sts)

Row 40: Sc2tog 2 times, sc in each st across, turn. (6 sts)

Row 41: Ch 1, sc in each st across to last 2 sts, sc2tog, turn. (5 sts)

Rows 42–43: Ch 1, sc in each st across, turn. Fasten off.

Back

With Color A, ch 47.

Row 1: Sc in second ch from hook and in each ch across, turn. (46 sts)

Rows 2–4: Ch 1, sc in each st across, turn. Fasten off.

Rows 5–22: Join Color B, ch 1, sc in each st across, turn.

Row 23: Ch 1, 2 sc in first st, sc to last st, 2 sc in last st, turn. (48 sts)

Row 24: Ch 1, 2 sc in first st, sc to last st, 2 sc in last st, turn. (50 sts)

Row 25: Sc2tog, sc to last 2 sts, sc2tog, turn. (48 sts)

Row 26: Sc2tog, sc to last 2 sts, sc2tog, turn. (46 sts)

Row 27: Sc2tog, sc to last 2 sts, sc2tog, turn. (44 sts)

Row 28: Sc2tog, sc to last 2 sts, sc2tog, turn. (42 sts)

Row 29: Sc2tog, sc to last 2 sts, sc2tog, turn. (40 sts)

Row 30: Sc2tog, sc to last 2 sts, sc2tog, turn. (38 sts)

Rows 31–43: Ch 1, sc in each st across, turn. Fasten off.

Body Assembly

With Right Sides together, sew shoulders to Back Panel.

Sew side seams together from bottom up to Row 25.

Sleeve (make 2)

With Color B, ch 33.

Row 1: Sc in second ch from hook and in each ch across, turn. (32)

Row 2: Ch 1, 2 sc in first st, sc in each st across, turn. (33 sts)

Row 3: Ch 1, 2 sc in first st, sc in each st across, turn. (34 sts)

Row 4: Ch 1, 2 sc in first st, sc in each st across, turn. (35 sts)

Row 5: Ch 1, 2 sc in first st, sc in each st across, turn. (36 sts)

Row 6: Ch 1, 2 sc in first st, sc in each st across, turn. (37 sts)

Row 7: Ch 1, 2 sc in first st, sc in each st across, turn. (38 sts)

Row 8: Place stitch marker on each end of row. Ch 1, sc in each st across, turn.

Rows 9–11: Ch 1, sc in each st across, turn.

Row 12: Sc2tog, sc in each st across, turn. (37 sts)

Row 13: Sc2tog, sc in each st across, turn. (36 sts)

Row 14: Sc2tog, sc in each st across, turn. (35 sts)

Rows 15–16: Ch 1, sc in each st across, turn.

Row 17: Sc2tog, sc in each st across, turn. (34 sts)

Rows 18–19: Ch 1, sc in each st across, turn.

Row 20: Sc2tog, sc in each st across, turn. (33 sts)

Rows 21–22: Ch 1, sc in each st across, turn.

Row 23: Sc2tog, sc in each st across, turn. (32 sts)

Rows 24–25: Ch 1, sc in each st across, turn.

Row 26: Sc2tog, sc in each st across, turn. (31 sts)

Rows 27–31: Ch 1, sc in each st across, turn.

Row 32: Sc2tog, sc in each st across to last 2 sts, sc2tog. Join Color A, fasten off Color B.

Rows 33–37: Ch 1, sc in each st across, turn. Fasten off.

9–12 months
Front Left
With Color A, ch 21.

Row 1 (RS): Sc in second ch from hook and in each ch across, turn. (20 sts)

Rows 2–4: Ch 1, sc in each st across, turn. Fasten off.

Rows 5–22: Join Color B, ch 1, sc in each st across, turn.

Row 23: Ch 1, sc in each st to last st, 2 sc in last st. (21 sts)

Row 24: Ch 1, 2sc in first st, sc in each st across, turn. (22 sts)

Row 25: Ch 1, sc in each st to last 2 sts, sc2tog (see Special Stitch), turn. (21 sts)

Row 26: Sc2tog, sc in each st across, turn. (20 sts)

Row 27: Ch 1, sc in each st to last 2 sts, sc2tog, turn. (19 sts)

Row 28: Sc2tog, sc in each st across, turn. (18 sts)

Row 29: Ch 1, sc in each st to last 2 sts, sc2tog, turn. (17 sts)

Row 30: Sc2tog, sc in each st across, turn. (16 sts)

Rows 31–38: Ch 1, sc in each st across, turn.

Row 39: Sc2tog, sc in each st across, turn. (15 sts)

Row 40: Ch 1, sc in each st to last 2 sts, sc2tog, turn. (14 sts)

Row 41: Sc2tog, sc in each st across, turn. (13 sts)

Row 42: Ch 1, sc in each st across to last 4 sts, sc2tog 2 times, turn. (11 sts)

Row 43: Sc2tog, sc in each st across, turn. (10 sts)

Row 44: Ch 1, sc in each st across to last 4 sts, sc2tog 2 times, turn. (8 sts)

Row 45: Sc2tog, sc in each st across, turn. (7 sts)

Rows 46–47: Ch 1, sc in each st across, turn. Fasten off.

Front Right
With Color A, ch 21.

Row 1 (RS): Sc in second ch from hook and in each ch across, turn. (20 sts)

Rows 2–4: Ch 1, sc in each st across, turn. Fasten off.

Rows 5–22: Join Color B, ch 1, sc in each st across, turn.

Row 23: Ch 1, 2 sc in first st, sc in each st across, turn. (21 sts)

Row 24: Ch 1, sc in each st to last st, 2 sc in last st, turn. (22 sts)

Row 25: Sc2tog, sc in each st across, turn. (21 sts)

Row 26: Ch 1, sc in each st to last 2 sts, sc2tog, turn. (20 sts)

Row 27: Sc2tog, sc in each st across, turn. (19 sts)

Row 28: Ch 1, sc in each st to last 2 sts, sc2tog, turn. (18 sts)

Row 29: Sc2tog, sc in each st across, turn. (17 sts)

Row 30: Ch 1, sc in each st to last 2 sts, sc2tog, turn. (16 sts)

Rows 31–38: Ch 1, sc in each st across, turn.

Row 39: Ch 1, sc in each st across to last 2 sts, sc2tog, turn. (15 sts)

Row 40: Sc2tog, sc in each st across, turn. (14 sts)

Row 41: Ch 1, sc in each st across to last 2 sts, sc2tog, turn. (13 sts)

Row 42: Sc2tog 2 times, sc in each st across, turn. (11 sts)

Row 43: Ch 1, sc in each st across to last 2 sts, sc2tog, turn. (10 sts)

Row 44: Sc2tog 2 times, sc in each st across, turn. (8 sts)

Row 45: Ch 1, sc in each st across to last 2 sts, sc2tog, turn. (7 sts)

Rows 46–47: Ch 1, sc in each st across, turn. Fasten off.

Back

With Color A, ch 51.

Row 1: Sc in second ch from hook and in each ch across, turn. (50 sts)

Rows 2–4: Ch 1, sc in each st across, turn. Fasten off.

Rows 5–26: Join Color B, ch 1, sc in each st across, turn.

Row 27: Ch 1, 2 sc in first st, sc to last st, 2 sc in last st, turn. (52 sts)

Row 28: Ch 1, 2 sc in first st, sc to last st, 2 sc in last st, turn. (54 sts)

Row 29: Sc2tog, sc to last 2 sts, sc2tog, turn. (52 sts)

Row 30: Sc2tog, sc to last 2 sts, sc2tog, turn. (50 sts)

Row 31: Sc2tog, sc to last 2 sts, sc2tog, turn. (48 sts)

Row 32: Sc2tog, sc to last 2 sts, sc2tog, turn. (46 sts)

Row 33: Sc2tog, sc to last 2 sts, sc2tog, turn. (44 sts)

Row 34: Sc2tog, sc to last 2 sts, sc2tog, turn. (42 sts)

Rows 35–47: Ch 1, sc in each st across, turn. Fasten off.

Body Assembly

With Right Sides together, sew shoulders to Back Panel.

Sew side seams together from bottom up to Row 29.

Sleeve (make 2)

With Color B, ch 35.

Row 1: Sc in second ch from hook and in each ch across, turn. (34 sts)

Row 2: Ch 1, 2 sc in first st, sc in each st across, turn. (35 sts)

Row 3: Ch 1, 2 sc in first st, sc in each st across, turn. (36 sts)

Row 4: Ch 1, 2 sc in first st, sc in each st across, turn. (37 sts)

Row 5: Ch 1, 2 sc in first st, sc in each st across, turn. (38 sts)

Row 6: Ch 1, 2 sc in first st, sc in each st across, turn. (39 sts)

Row 7: Ch 1, 2 sc in first st, sc in each st across, turn. (40 sts)

Row 8: Place stitch marker on each end of row. Ch 1, sc in each st across, turn.

Rows 9–11: Ch 1, sc in each st across, turn.

Row 12: Sc2tog, sc in each st across, turn. (39 sts)

Row 13: Sc2tog, sc in each st across, turn. (38 sts)

Row 14: Sc2tog, sc in each st across, turn. (37 sts)

Rows 15–16: Ch 1, sc in each st across, turn.

Row 17: Sc2tog, sc in each st across, turn. (36 sts)

Rows 18–19: Ch 1, sc in each st across, turn.

Row 20: Sc2tog, sc in each st across, turn. (35 sts)

Rows 21–22: Ch 1, sc in each st across, turn.

Row 23: Sc2tog, sc in each st across, turn. (34 sts)

Rows 24–25: Ch 1, sc in each st across, turn.

Row 26: Sc2tog, sc in each st across, turn. (33 sts)

Rows 27–35: Ch 1, sc in each st across, turn.

Row 36: Sc2tog, sc in each st across to last 2 sts, sc2tog, turn. Join Color A, fasten off Color B.

Rows 37–41: Ch 1, sc in each st across, turn. Fasten off.

Both Sizes

Sleeve Assembly

With Sweater RS facing, use stitch marker to attach sleeve to garment. Place the center of Row 1 in the shoulder seam. Use yarn needle to sew from center to right first, and then finish sleeve working center to left. Turn sweater WS out and finish sewing sleeve together.

Trim

Row 1: With sweater RS facing, join Color A on bottom left corner, ch 1, sc evenly across ends of rows around to bottom left corner, turn.

Row 2: Ch 2, dc in same st, dc in each st around to first sc of Row 1, turn.

Row 3: Ch 1, sc in each st across. Fasten off.

Finishing

Sew buttons onto left side evenly and securely. Slip through dc sts to finish.

Cupcake Toy

What can be sweeter than a cupcake toy? Use your scrap yarn to add "sprinkles" to the top and have fun making your own dozen cupcakes!

Yarn

Knit Picks Dishie; medium weight #4; 100% cotton; 3.5 oz. (100g)/190 yd. (174 m) per skein
- 1 skein each: 25399 Coffee, 25790 Begonia

Hook and Other Material
- US size F-5 (3.75 mm) crochet hook
- Yarn needle
- Poly-fil stuffing

Finished Measurements

4 in. (10 cm) wide

Gauge

5 sts x 3 rows = 1 in. (2.5 cm) in dc

Special Stitches

Front Post Double Crochet (FPdc). Yarn over, insert hook from front to back around post of st indicated, yarn over and pull up a loop (3 loops on hook), (yarn over and draw through 2 loops on hook) twice.

Back Post Double Crochet (BPdc). Yarn over, insert hook from back to front around post of st indicated, yarn over and pull up a loop (3 loops on hook), (yarn over and draw through 2 loops on hook) twice.

Single Crochet 2 Together (sc2tog). (Insert hook, yarn over, pull up loop) in each of the sts indicated, yarn over, draw through all loops on hook.

Pattern Note
- The beginning ch-2 of each round will not count as a stitch.

INSTRUCTIONS

Top

With Begonia, ch 4.

Rnd 1 (WS): 4 dc in first ch from hook, do not join. (4 sts)

Rnd 2: Working in the round, 2 FPdc (see Special Stitches) in each st around. (8 sts)

Rnd 3: * FPdc on next FPdc, 2 FPdc on next FPdc, rep from * around. (12 sts)

Rnd 4: * FPdc on next 2 FPdc, 2 FPdc on next FPdc, rep from * around. (16 sts)

Rnd 5: * FPdc on next 3 FPdc, 2 FPdc on next FPdc, rep from * around. (20 sts)

Rnd 6: * FPdc on next 4 FPdc, 2 FPdc on next FPdc, rep from * around. (24 sts)

Rnd 7: * FPdc on next 5 FPdc, 2 FPdc on next FPdc, rep from * around. (28 sts)

Rnds 8–10: FPdc on each FPdc around. Fasten off.

Use scrap yarn to add "sprinkles" around Top.

Ruffle Edge
Rnd 11: Ch 3,* sl st in next st, ch 3, rep from * around, join with sl st to first sl st. Fasten off.

Base
With Coffee, ch 2.
Rnd 1: 6 sc in second ch from hook, join with sl st to first sc. (6 st)
Rnd 2: Ch 1, 2 sc in each st around, join with sl st to first sc. (12 sts)
Rnd 3: Ch 1, sc in first sc, 2 sc in next sc, * sc in next st, 2 sc in next st, rep from * around, join with sl st to first sc. (18 sts)
Rnd 4: Ch 1, sc in first sc, sc in next sc, 2 sc in next st, * sc in next 2 sts, sc in next st, rep from * around, join with sl st to first sc. (24 sts)

Rnd 5: Ch 1, sc in first sc, sc in next 2 sts, 2 sc in next st, * sc in next 3 sts, 2 sc in next st, rep from * around, join with sl st to first sc. (30 sts)
Rnd 6: Ch 3, working in blo, dc in each st around, join with sl st to first dc.
Rnd 7: Ch 2, * FPdc in next st, BPdc (see Special Stitches) on next st, rep from * around, join with sl st to first FPdc.
Rnds 8–10: Ch 2, * FPdc on FPdc, BPdc on next FPdc, rep from * around, join with sl st to first FPdc. Fasten off.
Rnd 11: Ch 2, * FPdc on next 4 sts, BPdc 2 on next st, rep from * around, join with sl st to first FPdc. (36 sts) Fasten off.

Use yarn needle to sew (RS out) Top and Base together using the blo of Top and both stitches of Base; add Poly-fil stuffing before closing.

Sweetpea Topper

This lacy girl top is made in a weight #3 yarn and works up quickly. It is perfect for any afternoon out to the park or fun baby outing.

Sizes
3–6 months, 9–12 months

Yarn
Lion Brand Yarns Baby Soft; light weight #3; 60% acrylic, 40% nylon; 5 oz. (140 g)/459 yd. (420 m) per skein
- 2 skeins: 170 Sweet Pea
- 1 skein: 160 Lemonade

Hook and Other Materials
- US size G-6 (4 mm) crochet hook for 3–6 month size; H-8 (5 mm) for 9–12 month size
- Yarn needle
- Stitch markers

Finished Measurements
3–6 months: 8½ in. (22 cm) wide x 9½ in. (24 cm) long
9–12 months: 10 in. (25 cm) wide x 11 in. (28 cm) long

Gauge
3–6 months
With G-6 hook, 16 sts x 18 rows = 4 in. (10 cm) in sc
9–12 months
With H-8 hook, 14 sts x 17 rows = 4 in. (10 cm) in sc

Special Stitches
Shell. (Dc 2, ch 2, dc 2) in same st or sp indicated.
Picot. Ch 3, sl st to the first ch.

Pattern Notes
- The beginning ch-3 counts as the first dc.
- For size 9–12 months, use H-8 (5 mm) crochet hook or weight #4 yarn to naturally increase the size of the top.

INSTRUCTIONS

Note: For size 3–6 months, use G-6 (4 mm) crochet hook; for size 9–12 months, use H-8 (5 mm) crochet hook. The instructions are the same for both sizes.

Yoke

With Color A, ch 71.

Row 1: Sc in second ch from hook and in each across, sl st in last ch, turn. (70 sts)

Row 2: Ch 5 (buttonhole loop), dc in sl st, dc in next 5 sts, 2 dc in next st, * dc in next 6 sts, 2 dc in next st, rep from * across, turn. (80 sts)

Row 3: Ch 1, sc in first st, sc in next 6 sts, 2 sc in next st, * sc in next 7 sts, 2 sc in next st, rep from 8 across, leave buttonhole loop unworked, turn. (90 sts)

Row 4: Ch 3 (see Pattern Notes), dc in next 7 sts, 2 sc in next st, * dc in next 8 sts, 2 dc in next st, rep from * across, turn. (100 sts)

Row 5: Ch 1, sc in first st, sc in next 8 sts, 2 sc in next st, * sc in next 9 sts, 2 sc in next st, rep from * across, turn. (110 sts)

Row 6: Ch 3, dc in next 9 sts, 2 dc in next st, * dc in next 10 sts, 2 sc in next st, rep from * across, turn. (120 sts)

Body

Rnd 1: (*Note:* The round creates the armholes.) Ch 1, sc in first st, sc in next 11 sts, ch 18, sk 36 sts, sc in next 24 sts, ch 18, sk 36 sts, sc in next 12 sts, join with sl st to first sc.

Rnd 2: Ch 3, dc in each st and ch around, join with sl st to beg ch-3.

Rnd 3: Ch 1, sc in first st, * ch 5, sk 3 sts, sc in next st, rep from * until 3 sts remain, ch 5, sk 3, join with sl st to first sc.

Rnd 4: (Ch 3, dc, ch 2, dc 2) in same st, * sc in ch-5 sp **, shell (see Special Stitches) in next sc, rep from * around, ending last rep at **, shell in last sc, join with sl st to beg ch-3.

Rnd 5: Sl st to ch-2 sp, ch 1, sc in same sp, * ch-5, sc in ch-5 sp, ch 5 **, sc in ch-2 sp, rep from * around, ending last rep at **, join with sl st to first sc.

Rnd 6: (Ch 3, dc, ch 2, dc) in first st, * sc in ch-5 sp, ch 5, sc in next ch-5 sp **, shell in next sc, rep from * around, ending last rep at **, join with sl st to beg ch-3.

Rnd 7: Rep Rnd 5.

Rnds 8–17: Rep Rnds 6 and 7.

Rnd 18: (Ch 3, dc, ch 2, dc) in first st, * sc in ch-5 sp, ch 6, sc in next ch-5 sp **, shell in next sc, rep from * around, ending last rep at **, join with sl st to beg ch-3.

Rnd 19: Sl st to ch-2 sp, ch 1, sc in same sp, * ch-6, sc in ch-5 sp, ch 6 **, sc in ch-2 sp, rep from * around, ending last rep at **, join with sl st to first sc.

Rnds 20–23: Rep Rnds 18–19.

Rnd 24: Ch 1, sc in same st, (sc 3, picot [see Special Stitches], sc 3) in each ch-6 sp, sc in next sc, rep from * around, join with sl st in first sc. Fasten off.

Flower

With Color B, ch 2.

Rnd 1: 4 sc in second ch from hook, join with sl st to first st.

Rnd 2: Working in flo, (ch 4, sl st, ch 4, sl st) in first st, (sl st, ch 4, sl st, ch 4, sl st) in each st around, do not join.

Rnd 3: Working in blo of Rnd 1, (sl st, ch 4, sl st, ch 4, sl st) in each st around, do not join. Fasten off, leaving long end for sewing.

Sew button on back.

Use yarn needle to sew flower onto front center.

Baby Mat

Use this mat as a diaper-changing pad or even a nursery rug. It is fast and easy to create, and it's durable in the bulky yarn.

Yarn

Bernat Home Decor; bulky weight #5; 72% cotton, 28% nylon; 8.8 oz. (250 g)/317 yd. (290 m) per skein

- 1 skein each: Sweet Pea (A), Cream (B)

Hook

- US size I-9 (5.5 mm) crochet hook

Finished Measurements

25½ in. (65 cm) wide x 17 in. (43 cm) long

Gauge

12 sts x 6 rows = 4 in. (10 cm) in dc

Special Stitches

Shell. 5 dc in indicated stitch or sp.

Reverse Single Crochet (reverse sc). Insert hook from front to back in the next stitch to the right, yarn over, pull up loop, yarn over, and draw through 2 loops on hook.

Pattern Notes

- The beginning ch-4 counts as the first dc plus ch-1.
- The beginning ch-3 counts as the first dc.

INSTRUCTIONS

With Color A, ch 68.

Row 1: Sc in second ch from hook and in each across, turn. (67 sts)

Row 2: Ch 4 (see Pattern Notes), sk 1 st, dc in next st, * sk 2 sts, shell (see Special Stitches) in next st, sk 2 sts, dc in next st, ch 1, sk 1 st, dc in next st, rep from * across, turn.

Row 3: Ch 4, dc in next dc, * shell in center dc of next shell, sk next 2 dc on same shell, dc in next dc, ch 1, dc in next dc, rep from * across, ending with dc in ch-3 of turning ch-4, turn.

Rows 4–18: Rep Row 3.

Row 19: Ch 4, dc in next dc, * ch 1, sc in in the center dc of next shell, sk 2, dc in next dc, ch 1, dc in next dc, rep from * ending with dc in ch-2 of turning ch-4, turn.

Row 20: Ch 1, sc in each st and ch across. Do not turn. Join Color B, fasten off Color A.

Border

Rnd 1: Ch 1, sc evenly along ends of rows to Row 1, 3 sc in first st of Row 1, sc in each st across to last st, 3 sc in last st of Row 1, sc evenly along ends of rows to Row 20, 3 sc in first st of Row 20, sc in each st across to last st, 3 sc in last st, join with sl st to first sc.

Rnd 2: Ch 3 (see Pattern Notes), * dc in each st to the second sc of 3 sc in corner, (dc, ch 1, dc) in second st, rep from * until fourth corner is complete, dc in each st across, join with sl st to beg ch-3.

Rnds 3–5: Ch 3 (see Pattern Notes), * dc in each st to the ch-1 sp in corner, (dc, ch 1, dc) in ch-1 sp, rep from * until fourth corner is complete, dc in each st across, join with sl st to beg ch-3.

Rnd 6: Ch 1, sc in each st, 3 sc in each ch-1 sp in corners, join with sl st in first sc. Fasten off.

Rnd 7: With Color A, join in any corner st, ch 1, reverse sc (see Special Stitches) in each st around, join with sl st to first sc. Fasten off.

Jelly Bean Car Seat Cover

There's always something creative to crochet for babies, and it's even better when it has multiple functions. Cover your baby from the elements outside, and then use the blanket as needed inside. Mix and match colors and use your scrap yarn!

Yarn

Knit Picks Mighty Stitch; medium weight #4; 80% acrylic, 20% superwash wool; 3.5 oz. (100 g)/208 yd. (190 m) per skein
- 1 skein each: 26822 Conch, 26810 Canary, 26830 Sky, 26820 Silver, 26807 White

Hook and Other Materials
- US size I-9 (5.5 mm) crochet hook
- Yarn needle
- 2 buttons (2 in./5 cm)

Finished Measurements

28 in. (71 cm) wide x 44 in. (112 cm) long

Gauge

16 sts x 8 rows = 4 in. (10 cm) in dc

Special Stitch

Single Crochet 2 Together (sc2tog). (Insert hook, yarn over, pull up loop) in each of the sts indicated, yarn over, draw through all loops on hook.

Pattern Note
- When changing colors, complete the stitch until the last pull through; drop working yarn, pull through next color as last pull through to complete color change, and finish stitch.

INSTRUCTIONS

With Silver, ch 106.

Row 1: Dc in fourth ch from hook and in each st across, turn.

Row 2: Ch 1, (sc, hdc, dc) in first st, sk 2 sts, * (sc, hdc, dc) in next st, sk 2 sts, rep from * across, ending with sc in the last st. Join Conch, fasten off Silver (see Pattern Note).

Rows 3–9: Rep Row 2. Join Canary, fasten off Conch.

Rows 10–16: Rep Row 2. Join White, fasten off Canary.

Rows 17–23: Rep Row 2. Join Sky, fasten off White.

Rows 24–30: Rep Row 2. Join Silver, fasten off Sky.

Rows 31–37: Rep Row 2. Join Conch, fasten off Silver.

Rows 38–135: Rep Rows 3–37, ending on Row 30.

Rows 136–137: With Silver, rep Row 2. Do not turn.

Trim

Rnd 1: (Continue with Silver) Ch 1, sc evenly along ends of rows to Row 1, 3 sc in first st of Row 1, sc across Row 1 to last st, 3 sc in last st, sc evenly along ends of rows to Row 137, 3 sc in first st of Row 137, sc across Row 137 to last st, 3 sc in last st, join with sl st to first st. Fasten off.

Strap (make 2)

With Silver, ch 11.

Row 1: Sc in second ch from hook and in each across, turn. (10 sts)

Rows 2–18: Ch 1, sc in each st across, turn.

Row 19: Ch 1, sc in first st, sc in next 2 sts, ch 4, sk 4 sts, sc in last 3 sts, turn.

Row 20: Ch 1, sc in each st and ch across, turn.

Row 21: Sc2tog (see Special Stitch), sc in next 6 sts, sc2tog, turn.

Row 22: Sc2tog, sc in next 4 sts, sc2tog. Fasten off.

Use yarn needle to sew straps over the centerfold of blanket. Sew button in place so buttonhole slips over.

Lovey-Dovey Blanket

A quick-to-crochet blanket pattern is a nursery must-have. This colorblock blanket has two sections that bring just the right amount of character.

Yarn

Knit Picks Billow; bulky weight #5; 100% cotton; 3.5 oz. (100 g)/120 yd. (110 m) per skein
- 3 skeins each: 26222 Natural (A)
- 2 skeins each: 26226 Comfrey (B), 26237 Turmeric (C), 26234 Sagebrush (D)

Hook and Other Materials
- US size K-10½ (6.5 mm) crochet hook
- Yarn needle

Finished Measurements

29 in. (74 cm) wide x 38 in. (97 cm) long

Gauge

12 sts x 6 rows = 4 in. (10 cm) in V-st/Dc pattern

Special Stitches

Treble 3 Together (tr3tog). Yarn over twice, pull up a loop in next st, yarn over, (pull through first 2 loops) twice, [yarn over twice, pull up a loop in the next st, (yarn over and draw through first 2 loops) twice], yarn over pull through all loops on hook (counts as 1 tr).

Treble Double Crochet 2 Together (trdc2tog). Yarn over twice, pull up a loop in next st, (pull through first 2 loops) twice, leave loop on hook, yarn over, pull up a loop in next st, yarn over and draw through first 2 loops, yarn over, pull through all loops on hook (counts as 1 dc).

Double Crochet Treble 2 Together (dctr2tog). Yarn over, pull up a loop in next st, yarn over and draw through first 2 loops, leave loop on hook, yarn over twice, pull up a loop in next st, (pull through first 2 loops) twice, yarn over, pull through all loops on hook (counts as 1 dc).

Pattern Note
- When changing colors, complete the stitch until the last pull through; drop working yarn, pull through next color as last pull through to complete color change, and finish stitch.

INSTRUCTIONS

Chevron Panel

With Color A, ch 46.

Row 1 (RS): 2 sc in second ch from hook, sc in next 4 chs, sk 2 chs, sc in next 4 chs, * 3 sc in next ch, sc in next 4 chs, sk 2 chs, sc in next 4 chs, rep from * across, 2 sc in last ch, turn.

Row 2: Ch 1, 2 sc in in first sc, sc in next 4 sc, sk 2 sc, sc in next 4 sc, * 2 sc in next sc, sc in next 4 sc, sk 2 sc, sc in next 4 sc, rep from * across, 2 sc in last sc, turn.

Rows 3–4: Rep Row 2. Join Color B, fasten off Color A (see Pattern Note).

Rows 5–6: Rep Row 2. Join Color A, fasten off Color B.

Rows 7–10: Rep Row 2. Join Color C, fasten off Color A.

Rows 11–12: Rep Row 2. Join Color A, fasten off Color C.

Rows 13–14: Rep Row 2. Join Color D, fasten off Color A.

Rows 15–16: Rep Row 2. Join Color A, fasten off Color B.

Rows 17–64: Rep Rows 2–16, ending on Row 6.

Row 65: Ch 1, sc in first st, * sc in next st, hdc in next dc, dc in next st, tr3tog (see Special Stitches), dc in next st, hdc in next 2 sts, sc in next st **, sl st in next st, rep from * across, ending last rep at **, sc in last st, turn. Fasten off.

Row 1 (Finishing Row): Join on RS, ch 4, trdc2tog (see Special Stitches), dc in next st, hdc in next st (sc, sl st in ch-sp), * sc in next st, hdc in next st, dc in next st, tr3tog, dc in next st, hdc in next 2 sts, (sc, sl st) in ch-sp, rep from * to last ch-sp, sc in next st, hdc in next st, dc in next st, dctr2tog (see Special Stitches), dc in same st, turn. Fasten off.

Side Panel

Row 1: Join Color A in RS edge of Chevron Panel, use ends of rows as stitches, ch 3, sk 2 sts, * (dc, ch 1, dc) in next st, sk 2 sts, rep from * across, dc in last st, turn.

Row 2: Ch 3, dc in each st and ch across, turn.

Row 3: Ch 3, sk 2 sts, (dc, ch 1, dc) in next st, sk 2 sts, rep from * across, dc in last st, turn. Fasten off Color A, join Color B.

Row 4: Rep Row 2.

Row 5: Rep Row 3.

Row 6: Rep Row 2. Join Color C, fasten off Color B.

Row 7: Rep Row 3.

Row 8: Rep Row 2.

Row 9: Rep Row 3. Join Color D, fasten off Color C.

Row 10: Rep Row 2.

Row 11: Rep Row 3.

Row 12: Rep Row 2. Join Color A, fasten off Color D.

Row 13: Rep Row 3.

Row 14: Rep Row 2.

Row 15: Rep Row 3. Join Color B, fasten off Color A.

Rows 16–36: Rep Rows 2 and 3, ending on Row 2. Fasten off Color B.

Trim

Rnd 1: Join Color A in top right corner, ch 6 (counts as first dc and ch 3), dc in same st, * (2 dc in next st, sk 1 st) across to next corner, (dc, ch 3, dc) in corner, using ends of rows as sts, (2 dc in next st, sk 1 st) across to next corner **, (dc, ch 3, dc) in corner, rep from * around, ending last rep at **, join with sl st to beg ch-3. Fasten off.

Rnd 2: Join in ch-3 sp in corner, ch 6, dc in same sp, * 2 dc in each ch-1 sp ** to ch-3 sp in corner (dc, ch 3, dc) in ch-3 sp, rep from * around, ending last rep at **, join with sl st to beg ch-3. Fasten off.

Rnd 3: Join in ch-3 sp, ch 1, * (sc, ch 3, sc) in ch-3 sp, sc in each st and ch-sp around, rep from * around, join with sl st in first sc. Fasten off.

Rnd 4: Join Color B, in ch-3 sp, ch 1, * 3 sc in ch-3 sp, sc in each st across, rep from * around, join with sl st to first sc. Fasten off.

Darling Daisy Vest

This vest is beyond easy! Both front sides are made from the same triangle pattern and then sewn onto the back to create the sweetest lacy vest.

Sizes
3–6 months, 9–12 months

Yarn
Knit Picks Comfy Sport; fine weight #2; 75% pima cotton, 25% acrylic; 1.75 oz. (50 g)/136 yd. (124 m) per skein
- 2 skeins: 24429 Ivory

Hook and Other Materials
- US size F (3.75 mm) crochet hook
- Yarn needle
- Stitch markers
- 1 button (1 in./2.5 cm)
- Sewing needle and matching thread

Finished Measurements
3–6 months: 8 in. (20 cm) wide x 8 in. (20 cm) long
9–12 months: 10 in. (25 cm) wide x 10 in. (25 cm) long

Gauge
17 sts x 10 rows = 4 in. (10 cm) in dc

Pattern Notes
- The beginning ch-6 counts as the first dc plus ch-3.
- The beginning ch-4 counts as the first dc plus ch-1.
- The beginning ch-3 counts as the first dc.

INSTRUCTIONS
3–6 months
Triangle Panel (make 2)
Ch 5, join with sl st to first ch.
Row 1: Ch 6 (see Pattern Notes), dc in ring, * ch 3, dc in ring, rep 2 more times, turn. (4 ch-3 sp, 5 dc)
Row 2: Ch 6, 4 dc in next dc, ch 3, dc in next dc, ch 3, 3 dc in next 3 dc, ch 3, dc in ch-4 of turning ch-6, turn.

Row 3: Ch 6, * 2 dc in next dc, dc in next dc, 2 dc in next dc, ch 3, dc in next dc **, ch 3, rep from * across, ending last rep at **, turn.
Row 4: Ch 4 (see Pattern Notes), dc in same st, * ch 3, 2 dc in next dc, dc in next 3 dc, 2 dc in next dc, ch 3 **, (dc, ch 1, dc, ch 1, dc) in next dc, rep from * ending last rep at **, (dc, ch 1, dc) in last dc, turn.
Row 5: Ch 6, 3 dc in next dc, ch 3, sk 1 dc, dc 5, sk 1 dc, ch 3, 3 dc in next dc, ch 3, dc in next dc, ch 3, 3 dc in next dc, ch 3, sk 1 dc, dc 5, sk 1 dc, 3 dc in next dc, ch 3, dc in last dc, turn.

Row 6: Ch 6, 2 dc in next dc, dc in next st, 2 dc in next dc, ch 3, sk 1 dc, dc in next 3 dc, sk 1 dc, ch 3, 2 dc in next dc, dc in next st, 2 dc in next st, ch 3, dc in next dc, ch 3, 2 dc in next dc, dc in next dc, 2 dc in next st, ch 3, sk 1 dc, dc in next 3 dc, sk 1 dc, ch 3, 2 dc in next dc, dc in next st, 2 dc in next st, ch 3, dc in last st, turn.

Row 7: Ch 4, dc in same st, ch 3, 2 dc in next dc, dc in next 3 dc, 2 dc in next st, ch 3, sk 1 dc, dc in next dc, sk 1 dc, ch 3, 2 dc in next st, dc in next 3 sts, 2 dc in next st, ch 3, (dc, ch 1, dc, ch 1, dc) in next dc, ch 3, 2 dc in next st, dc in next 3 sts, 2 dc in next st, ch 3, sk 1 st, dc in next st, 1, sk 1 st, ch 3, 2 dc in next st, dc in next 3 sts, 2 dc in next st, ch 3, dc in next st, ch 1, dc in last dc, turn.

Row 8: Ch 6, 3 dc in next dc, ch 3, sk 1 dc, dc in next 5 sts, sk 1 dc, ch 3, 3 dc in next dc, ch 3, sk 1 st, dc in next 5 sts, sk 1 dc, ch 3, 3 dc in next st, (ch 3, dc in next st, ch 3) twice, sk 1 st, dc in next 5 sts, sk 1 st, ch 3, 3 dc in next dc, ch 3, sk 1 st, dc in next 5 sts, sk 1 st, ch 3, 3 dc in next dc, ch 3, dc in last st, turn.

Row 9: Ch 6, 2 dc in next st, dc in next st, 2 dc in next dc, ch 3, sk 1 st, dc in next 3 sts, sk 1 st, ch 3, [2 dc in next st, dc in next st, 2 dc in next st, ch 3, sk 1 st, dc in next 3 sts, sk 1 st, ch 3] 3 times, 2 dc in next st, dc in next st, 2 dc in next st, ch 3, dc in last st, turn.

Back Panel

Ch 35.

Row 1: Sc in second ch from hook and in each across, turn. (34 sts)

Row 2: Ch 3 (see Pattern Notes), dc in each st across, turn.

Row 3: Ch 3, dc in next st, * ch 1, sk 1 st, dc in next st, rep across, turn.

Row 4: Ch 3, dc in each st around, turn.

Rows 5–8: Rep Rows 3 and 4.

Rows 9–21: Ch 3, dc in each st around, turn.

Assembly

Use yarn needle and sew each Triangle Panel to Back Panel 4 in. from bottom to top.

Sew the top to the Back Panel.

Armholes Trim

Join yarn at seam, ch 1, sc evenly across ends of rows, join with sl st to first sc. Fasten off.

Finishing

Securely sew button on Right Front Triangle, slip Left Front over.

9–12 months

Triangle Panel (make 2)

Repeat Rows 1–9 from 3–6 months.

Row 10: Ch 4, dc in same st, [2 dc in next st, dc in next 3 sts, 2 dc in next st, ch 3, sk 1 st, dc in next st, sk 1 st, ch 3] twice, 2 dc in next st, dc in next 3 sts, 2 dc in next st, ch 3, (dc, ch 1, dc, ch 1, dc) in next dc, ch 3, [2 dc in next st, dc in next 3 sts, 2 dc in next st, ch 3, sk 1 st, dc in next st, sk 1 st, ch 3] twice, 2 dc in next st, dc in next 3 sts, 2 dc in next st, ch 3, (dc, ch 1, dc) in last st. Fasten off.

Back Panel

Ch 43.

Row 1: Sc in second ch from hook and in each across, turn. (42 sts)

Row 2: Ch 3 (see Pattern Notes), dc in each st across, turn.

Row 3: Ch 3, dc in next st, * ch 1, sk 1 st, dc in next st, rep from * across, turn.

Row 4: Ch 3, dc in each st around, turn.

Rows 5–8: Rep Rows 3 and 4.

Rows 9–26: Ch 3, dc in each st around, turn.

Assembly

Use yarn needle and sew each Triangle Panel to Back Panel 4½ in. from bottom to top.

Sew the top to Back Panel.

Armholes Trim

Join yarn at seam, ch 1, sc evenly across ends of rows, join with sl st to first sc. Fasten off.

Finishing

Securely sew button on Right Front Triangle, slip Left Front over.

Big Champ Hooded Jacket

A variety of stripes gives interest to this adorable hooded jacket. It is crocheted with basic stitches and medium-weight yarn.

Sizes
3–6 months, 9–12 months

Yarn
Lion Brand Yarn Vanna's Choice; medium weight #4; 100% acrylic; 3.5 oz. (100 g)/170 yd. (156 m) per skein

- 2 skeins: 860-180E Cranberry (A)
- 1 skein each: 860-150 Pale Gray (B), 860-100 White (C)

Hook and Other Materials

- US size I-9 (5.5 mm) crochet hook
- Yarn needle
- Stitch markers
- 7 buttons (1 in./2.5 cm)
- Sewing needle and matching thread

Finished Measurements
3–6 months: 8 in. (20 cm) wide x 8¾ in. (22 cm) long
9–12 months: 10 in. (25 cm) wide x 10¾ in. (27 cm) long

Gauge
14 sts x 16 rows = 4 in. (10 cm) in sc

Special Stitch
Whipstitch. Holding the right sides together, insert needle front to back through both pieces. Bring needle over seam back to front and insert front to back; repeat.

Pattern Note

- The jacket is made in joined sections. The base is made until it reaches under the arms. Then it splits into three sections and is worked separately: Right Side, Back, and Left Side. Next, it is sewn together in preparation for the Hood and Sleeves. After the hood is added, the trim is completed. It is finished by crocheting the sleeves and sewing the buttons in place.

INSTRUCTIONS

3–6 months

Base

With Color A, ch 71.

Row 1: Sc in second ch from hook and in each across, turn. (70 sts)

Rows 2–10: Ch 1, sc in each st across, turn. Join Color B, fasten off Color A.

Rows 11–12: Ch 1, sc in each st across, turn. Join Color C, fasten off Color B.

Rows 13–14: Ch 1, sc in each st across, turn. Join Color B, fasten off Color C.

Rows 15–19: Rep Rows 11–14.

Working directly into Right Side

Row 1: (Use Color B) Ch 1, sc in next 17 sts, turn.

Row 2: Ch 1, sc in each st across, turn. Join Color C, fasten off Color B.

Rows 3–4: Ch 1, sc in each st across, turn. Join Color B, fasten off Color C.

Rows 5–6: Ch 1, sc in each st across, turn. Join Color C, fasten off Color B.

Rows 7–14: Rep Rows 3–6 twice. Fasten off.

Back

Row 1: Join Color B in next unworked st on Row 22, ch 1, sc in next 36 sts, turn.

Row 2: Ch 1, sc in each st across, turn. Join Color C, fasten off Color B.

Rows 3–4: Ch 1, sc in each st across, turn. Join Color B, fasten off Color C.

Rows 5–6: Ch 1, sc in each st across, turn. Join Color C, fasten off Color B.

Rows 7–14: Rep Rows 3–6 twice. Fasten off.

Left Side

Row 1: Join Color B in next unworked st on Row 22, ch 1, sc in next 17 sts, turn.

Row 2: Ch 1, sc in each st across, turn. Join Color C, fasten off Color B.

Rows 3–4: Ch 1, sc in each st across, turn. Join Color B, fasten off Color C.

Rows 5–6: Ch 1, sc in each st across, turn. Join Color C, fasten off Color B.

Rows 7–14: Rep Rows 3–6 twice. Fasten off.

Assembly

Use yarn needle to sew shoulders 6 sts in from each side using whipstitch (see Special Stitch).

Sew sides together, leaving 4 in. open for armhole.

Hood

Row 1: Join Color B in end of Row 14 on Left Side, sc in each st across, across Back and across Row 14 on Right Side.

Rows 2–24: Ch 1, sc in each st across, turn. Fasten off.

Sew top of hood together with whipstitch.

Trim

Row 1: Join Color B in bottom Left corner, ch 1, sc evenly across Left Side edge, around Hood and across Right Side edge, turn.

Row 2: Ch 1, sc in next 5 sts, ch 2, sk 2 [sc in next 2 sts, ch 2, sk 2] 7 times, sc across to end, turn.

Row 3: Ch 1, sc in each st and ch-sp across, sl st in last st. Do not turn.

Bottom Trim

Row 1: Working right into Bottom Trim, sl st in each st across bottom, sl st in first st on Row 3 Trim, join with sl st to first sl st of Row 3 Trim. Fasten off.

Sleeves (repeat on each side)

Rnd 1: Join Color B at bottom of armhole, sc evenly across ends of rows, turn.

Rnd 2: Ch 1, sc in each st across, turn. Join Color C, fasten off Color B.

Rnds 3–4: Ch 1, sc in each st across, turn. Join Color B, fasten off Color C.

Rnds 5–6: Ch 1, sc in each st across, turn. Join Color C, fasten off Color B.

Rnds 7–22: Rep Rnds 3–6. Fasten off.

Turn garment WS out, sew sleeves together. Turn RS out.

Trim

Rnd 1: Join Color A in seam, ch 1, sc in each st around, join with sl st to first sc.

Rnd 2: Ch 1, sc in each st around, join with sl st to first sc. Fasten off.

Note: You can add more rounds here if you want to create a cuff. Simply repeat Rnd 2 and fasten off when desired cuff length is obtained. This will make sleeve length adjustable.

Finishing

Securely sew buttons opposite buttonholes.

9–12 months
Base

With Color A, ch 77.

Row 1: Sc in second ch from hook and in each across, turn. (76 sts)

Rows 2–14: Ch 1, sc in each st across, turn. Join Color B, fasten off Color A.

Rows 15–16: Ch 1, sc in each st across, turn. Join Color C, fasten off Color B.

Rows 17–18: Ch 1, sc in each st across, turn. Join Color B, fasten off Color C.

Rows 19–22: Rep Rows 15–18.

Working directly into Right Side

Row 1: (Use Color B) Ch 1, sc in next 19 sts, turn.

Row 2: Ch 1, sc in each st across, turn. Join Color C, fasten off Color B.

Rows 3–4: Ch 1, sc in each st across, turn. Join Color B, fasten off Color C.

Rows 5–6: Ch 1, sc in each st across, turn. Join Color C, fasten off Color B.

Rows 7–8: Ch 1, sc in each st across, turn. Join Color B, fasten off Color C.

Rows 9–16: Rep Rows 5–8 twice. Fasten off.

Back

Row 1: Join Color B in next unworked st on Row 22, ch 1, sc in next 38 sts, turn.

Row 2: Ch 1, sc in each st across, turn. Join Color C, fasten off Color B.

Rows 3–4: Ch 1, sc in each st across, turn. Join Color B, fasten off Color C.

Rows 5–6: Ch 1, sc in each st across, turn. Join Color C, fasten off Color B.

Rows 7–8: Ch 1, sc in each st across, turn. Join Color B, fasten off Color C.

Rows 9–16: Rep Rows 5–8 twice. Fasten off.

Left Side

Row 1: Join Color B in next unworked st on Row 22, ch 1, sc in next 19 sts, turn.

Row 2: Ch 1, sc in each st across, turn. Join Color C, fasten off Color B.

Rows 3–4: Ch 1, sc in each st across, turn. Join Color B, fasten off Color C.

Rows 5–6: Ch 1, sc in each st across, turn. Join Color C, fasten off Color B.

Rows 7–8: Ch 1, sc in each st across, turn. Join Color B, fasten off Color C.

Rows 9–16: Rep Rows 5–8 twice. Fasten off.

Assembly

Use a yarn needle to sew 7 sts in from each side using whipstitch.

Sew sides together, leaving 4½ in. open for armhole.

Hood

Row 1: Join Color B on end of Row 14 on Left Side, sc in each st across, across Back and across Row 14 on Right Side.

Rows 2–26: Ch 1, sc in each st across, turn. Fasten off.

Sew top of hood together with whipstitch.

Trim

Row 1: Join Color B in bottom Left corner, ch 1, sc evenly across Left Side edge, around Hood and across Right Side edge, turn.

Row 2: Ch 1, sc in next 7 sts, ch 2, sk 2 [sc in next 2 sts, ch 2, sk 2] 7 times, sc across to end, turn.

Row 3: Ch 1, sc in each st and ch-sp across, sl st in last st. Do not turn.

Bottom Trim

Row 1: Working right into Bottom Trim, sl st in each st across bottom, sl st in first st on Row 3 Trim, join with sl st to first st st of Row 3 Trim. Fasten off.

Sleeves (repeat on each side)

Rnd 1: Join Color B at bottom of armhole, sc evenly across ends of rows, turn.

Rnd 2: Ch 1, sc in each st across, turn. Join Color C, fasten off Color B.

Rnds 3–4: Ch 1, sc in each st across, turn. Join Color B, fasten off Color C.

Rnds 5–6: Ch 1, sc in each st across, turn. Join Color C, fasten off Color B.

Rnds 7–26: Rep Rnds 3–6. Fasten off.

Turn garment WS out; sew sleeves together. Turn RS out.

Trim

Rnd 1: Join Color A in seam, ch 1, sc in each st around, join with sl st to first sc.

Rnd 2: Ch 1, sc in each st around, join with sl st to first sc. Fasten off.

Note: You can add more rounds here if you want to create a cuff. Simply repeat Rnd 2 and fasten off when desired cuff length is obtained. This will make sleeve length adjustable.

Finishing

Securely sew buttons opposite buttonholes.

Half-Pint Loafers

Easy, adorable, and great for boys or girls . . . and don't forget that pop of color!

Sizes
Small, Medium

Yarn
Premier Yarns Everyday Collection; medium
  weight #4; 100% acrylic; 4 oz. (113
  g)/203 yd. (186 m) per skein
- 1 skein each: ED100-23 Mist (A), ED100-
  16 Kiwi (B)

Hook and Other Materials
- US size F-6 (3.75 mm) crochet hook
- Yarn needle
- 4 stitch markers

Finished Measurements
Small: 2 in. (5 cm) wide x 3 in. (7.5 cm)
  long
Medium: 2 in. (5 cm) wide x 3½ in. (9 cm)
  long

Gauge
5 sts x 3 rows = 1 in. (2.5 cm) in hdc

Special Stitches
Double Crochet 2 Together (dc2tog). Yarn over, pull up a loop in next st, yarn
  over, pull through first 2 loops, yarn over, pull up a loop in the next stitch, yarn
  over and draw through first 2 loops, yarn over, pull through all loops on hook
  (counts as 1 dc).
Single Crochet 2 Together (sc2tog). Pull up a loop in each of next 2 sc, yarn over
  and draw through all 3 loops on hook (counts as 1 sc).
Half Double Crochet 2 Together (hdc2tog). Yarn over, pull up a loop in st, yarn
  over, pull up a loop in next st, yarn over, pull through all loops on hook (counts
  as 1 hdc).

INSTRUCTIONS

Small

Sole (make 2 in each color)

Ch 8.

Rnd 1: Sc in second ch from hook and in next 5 chs, 4 sc in last ch, working in free loops of beginning ch, sc in next 5 chs, 3 sc in last ch, join with sl st to first sc. (18 sts)

Rnd 2: Ch 1, sc in same st as joining, sc in next 2 sts, hdc in next 3 sts, 2 dc in next st, 3 dc in next 2 sts, 2 dc in next st, hdc in next 3 sts, sc in last 2 sts, 2 sc in last 3 sts, join with sl st to first sc. (27 sts)

Rnd 3: Ch 1, hdc in same st as joining, hdc in next 5 sts, (hdc in next st, 2 hdc in next st) 4 times, hdc in next 5 sts, [hdc in next st (mark the first hdc), 2 hdc in next st] 3 times, join with sl st to first hdc. Fasten off. (34 sts)

Rnd 4: Join Color B in top loop of sl st, sl st in next 2 sts, hdc in next, dc in each 4 sc, hdc in next st, sl st in each st to end, join with sl st to first sl st. Fasten off.

Sl st soles together.

Toes

Rnd 1: Join Color A in marked stitch from Rnd 3, ch 1, working in back loops only, hdc in each st, join with sl st to first hdc.

Rnd 2: Ch 1, hdc in each st around, join with sl st to first hdc.

Rnd 3: Ch 1, sc in same st as joining, sc in next 3 sts, dc2tog (see Special Stitches) 8 times, sc in next 4 sts, hdc to end, join with sl st to first st to join.

Rnd 4: Ch 1, sc in same st as joining, sc in next st, sc2tog (see Special Stitches), hdc2tog (see Special Stitches), dc2tog 2 times, hdc2tog, sc2tog, sc in each st to end, join with sl st to first st to join.

Rnd 5: Ch 1, sl st in same st as joining, sl st in next 2 sts, sc in next 4 sts, sl st to end, join with sl st to beg sl st. Fasten off.

Rnd 6: Join Color B in top loop of sl st, sl st in next 2 sts, hdc in next, dc in each 4 sc, hdc in next st, sl st in each st to end, join with sl st to first sl st. Fasten off.

Medium

Sole (make 2 in each color)

Ch 10.

Rnd 1: Sc in second ch from hook and in next 7 chs, 4 sc in last ch, working in free loops of beginning ch, sc in next 7 chs, 3 sc in last ch, join with sl st to first sc. (22 sts)

Rnd 2: Ch 1, sc in same st as joining, sc in next 4 sts, hdc in next 3 sts, 2 dc in next st, 3 dc in next 2 sts, 2 dc in next st, hdc in next 3 sts, sc in last 4 sts, 2 sc in last 3 sts, join with sl st to first sc. (31 sts)

Rnd 3: Ch 1, hdc in same st as joining, hdc in next 7 sts, (hdc in next st, 2 hdc in next st) 4 times, hdc in next 7 sts, [hdc in next st (mark the first hdc), 2 hdc in next st] 3 times, join with sl st to first hdc. Fasten off. (38 sts)

Sl st soles together.

Toes

Rnd 1: Join Color A in marked stitch from Rnd 3, ch 1, working in back loops only, hdc in each st, join with sl st to first hdc.

Rnd 2: Ch 1, hdc in each st around, join with sl st to first hdc.

Rnd 3: Ch 1, sc in same st as joining, sc in next 5 sts, dc2tog (see Special Stitches) 8 times, sc in next 6 sts, hdc to end, join with sl st to first st to join. (24 sts)

Rnd 4: Ch 1, sc in same st as joining, sc in next 3 sts, sc2tog (see Special Stitches), hdc2tog (see Special Stitches), dc2tog 2 times, hdc2tog, sc2tog, sc in each st to end, join with sl st to first st to join. (18 sts)

Rnd 5: Ch 1, sl st in same st as joining, sl st in next 3 sts, sc in next 4 sts, sl st to end, join with sl st to beg sl st. Fasten off.

Rnd 6: Join Color B in top loop of sl st, sl st in next 3 sts, hdc in next, dc in each 4 sc, hdc in next st, sl st in each st to end, join with sl st to first sl st. Fasten off.

Precious Princess Slippers

These tiny footwear are perfect for those last-minute gifts. Keep those little feet warm and in style!

Sizes
Small, Medium

Yarn
Plymouth Yarn Encore Worsted; medium weight #4; 75% acrylic, 25% wool; 3.5 oz. (100 g)/200 yd. (183 m) per skein
- 1 skein each: 9801 Dove (A), 208 White (B), 1317 Vacation Blues (C)

Hook and Other Materials
- US size F-5 (3.75 mm) crochet hook
- Yarn needle
- 4 stitch markers

Finished Measurements
Small: 2 in. (5 cm) wide x 3 in. (7.5 cm) long
Medium: 2 in. (5 cm) wide x 3½ in. (9 cm) long

Gauge
8 sts x 9 rows = 2 in. (5 cm) in sc

Special Stitches
Single Crochet 2 Together (sc2tog). (Insert hook, yarn over, pull up loop) in each of the sts indicated, yarn over, draw through all loops on hook.
Double Crochet 2 Together (dc2tog). Yarn over, pull up a loop in next st, yarn over, pull through first 2 loops, yarn over, pull up a loop in the next stitch, yarn over and draw through first 2 loops, yarn over, pull through all loops on hook (counts as 1 dc).

Pattern Note
- The beginning ch-3 counts as the first dc.

INSTRUCTIONS
Small
Sole (make 1 in Color A and Color B)
Rnd 1: Sc in second ch from hook and in each ch across to last ch, 4 hdc in last ch, working in free loops of beginning ch, sc in next 5 chs, 3 sc in next ch, join with sl st to first sc. (18 sts)

Rnd 2: Ch 1, sc in same st as joining and in next 3 sts, hdc in next 2 sts, 2 dc in each of next 4 sts, hdc in next 2 sts, sc in next 3 sts, 2 sc in each of last 3 sts, join with sl st to first st. (25 sts)

Rnd 3: Ch 2 (does not count as a st), hdc in same st as joining and in next 6 sts, 2 hdc in next st, (hdc in next st, 2 hdc in next st) 3 times, hdc in next 5 sts, (sc in next sc, 2 sc in next st) 3 times, join with sl st to first st. (32 sts)

Slip stitch soles together with Color C.

Toe
Rnd 1: Join Color A in marked stitch, ch 1, working in back loops only, sc in same st, sc in next 3 sts, (dc in next st, dc2tog) (see Special Stitches) 4 times, sc until 10 sts remain, dc in each st to end, join with sl st to first sc.

Rnd 2: Ch 1, sc in same st, sc in next 2 sts, dc2tog 5 times, sc in next 3 sts, hdc in next 2 sts, dc in each st to end, join with sl st to first sc.

Rnd 3: Ch 1, sc in same st, sc in each st until 10 sts remain, dc in each st to end, join with sl st to first sc. Fasten off.

Medium
Sole (make 1 sole in Color A and Color B)
Rnd 1: Sc in second ch from hook and in each ch across to last ch, 4 hdc in last ch, working in free loops of beginning ch, sc in next 7 chs, 3 sc in next ch, join with sl st to first sc. (22 sts)

Rnd 2: Ch 1, sc in same st as joining and in next 5 sts, hdc in next 2 sts, 2 dc in each of next 4 sts, hdc in next 2 sts, sc in next 5 sts, 2 sc in each of last 3 sts, join with sl st to first st. (29 sts)

Rnd 3: Ch 2 (does not count as a st), hdc in same st as joining and in next 8 sts, [hdc in next st (mark the first hdc with stitch marker), 2 hdc in next st] 4 times, hdc in next 7 sts, (sc in next st, 2 sc in next st) 3 times, join with sl st to first st. (36 sts) Fasten off.

Slip stitch soles together with Color C.

Toe
Rnd 1: Join Color A in marked stitch, ch 1, working in back loops only, sc in same st, sc in next 5 sts, (dc in next st, dc2tog) 4 times, sc until 10 sts remain, dc in each st to end, join with sl st to first sc.

Rnd 2: Ch 1, sc in same st, sc in next 3 sts, dc2tog 5 times, sc in next 4 sts, hdc in next 2 sts, dc in each st to end, join with sl st to first sc.

Rnd 3: Ch 1, sc in same st, sc in each st until 10 sts remain, dc in each st to end, join with sl st to first sc. Fasten off.

Both Sizes

Finishing

Left Ankle

Row 1: Count 11 sts around heel and join in next st, ch 3, dc in next 11 sts, turn.

Row 2: Ch 1, sc in each st around, ch 18.

(*Note:* Add or subtract chs as needed for exact fit on each Row 2 of Ankle.)

Row 3: Sl st in the fourth ch from hook to create button loop, sl st in each st across. Fasten off.

Right Ankle

Row 1: Count 11 sts around heel and join in next st, ch 3, dc in next 11 sts, turn.

Row 2: Ch 1, sc in each st around.

Row 3: Ch 1, sl st in each across, ch 18, sl st in fourth ch from hook to create button loop, sl st in each st across strap, sl st to first st on ankle. Fasten off.

Flower

With Color C, ch 2.

Rnd 1: Ch 3, sl st in second ch from hook, * ch 3, sl st in same center ch, rep from * around until 6 petals are complete. Fasten off, leaving long end for sewing.

Use yarn needle to sew flower opposite of closing strap.

How to Read the Patterns

*
Work instructions following * as many more times as indicated in addition to the first time.

( ) or [ ]
Work enclosed instructions as many times as specified by the number immediately following, or work all enclosed instructions in the stitch or space indicated. May also contain explanatory remarks.

Parentheses ( )
The number(s) given at the end of a row or round in the parentheses denote(s) the number of stitches or spaces you should have on that row or round.

Gauge
Exact gauge is essential for proper size. Before you begin your project, make the sample swatch given in the instructions for the pattern using the yarn and hook specified. After completing the swatch, measure it, counting the stitches and rows carefully. If your swatch is larger or smaller than specified, make another, changing hook size to get the correct gauge. Keep trying until you find the size hook that will give you the specified gauge.

Skill Level
Beginner: Projects for first-time crocheters using basic stitches. Minimal shaping.
Easy: Projects using yarn with basic stitches, repetitive stitch patterns, simple color changes, and simple shaping and finishing.
Intermediate: Projects using a variety of techniques, such as basic lace patterns or color patterns, midlevel shaping and finishing.
Experienced: Projects with intricate stitch patterns, techniques, and dimensions, such as nonrepeating patterns, multicolor techniques, fine threads, small hooks, detailed shaping, and refined finishing.

Materials
Items you will need to complete the patterns in this book include crochet hooks, stitch markers, pins, scissors, yarn, ruler, and a yarn needle.

Crochet Hooks
Each pattern will list the crochet hook needed for that project. Always use the same hook stated and check the gauge before starting the project. Change the hook size as necessary to obtain the correct gauge so that the project will be finished in the correct size.

Stitch Markers
Stitch markers are used to mark specific stitches in a pattern. If you do not have access to ready-made markers, use a piece of scrap yarn or even a bobby pin to mark the stitch.

Yarn
For each pattern, the specific yarn(s) and color(s) I used to crochet the pattern are given, along with how many skeins you'll need. Also included is each yarn's "yarn weight." You'll find this information on the label of every skein of yarn you buy, and it ranges from #0 lace weight to #7 jumbo weight. If you can't find the specific yarn I used or you'd like to use something else, knowing the yarn weight will let you pick another yarn that will have the same gauge.

Yarn Needle
The yarn needle is used to sew different pieces together and for weaving in ends.

Standard Yarn Weight System

Categories of yarn, gauge ranges, and recommended needle and hook sizes

Yarn Weight Symbol & Category Names	0 LACE	1 SUPER FINE	2 FINE	3 LIGHT	4 MEDIUM	5 BULKY	6 SUPER BULKY	7 JUMBO
Type of Yarns in Category	Fingering, 10-Count Crochet Thread	Sock, Fingering, Baby	Sport, Baby	DK, Light Worsted	Worsted, Afghan, Aran	Chunky, Craft, Rug	Bulky, Roving	Jumbo, Roving
Knit Gauge Range in Stockinette Stitch to 4 inches*	33–40 sts**	27–32 sts	23–26 sts	21–24 st	16–20 sts	12–15 sts	7–11 sts	6 sts and fewer
Recommended Needle in Metric Size Range	1.5–2.25 mm	2.25–3.25 mm	3.25–3.75 mm	3.75–4.5 mm	4.5–5.5 mm	5.5–8 mm	8–12.75 mm	12.75 mm and larger
Recommended Needle in U.S. Size Range	000 to 1	1 to 3	3 to 5	5 to 7	7 to 9	9 to 11	11 to 17	17 and larger
Crochet Gauge Ranges in Single Crochet to 4 inches*	32–42 double crochets**	21–32 sts	16–20 sts	12–17 sts	11–14 sts	8–11 sts	7–9 sts	6 sts and fewer
Recommended Hook in Metric Size Range	Steel*** 1.6–1.4 mm Regular hook 2.25 mm	2.25–3.5 mm	3.5–4.5 mm	4.5–5.5 mm	5.5–6.5 mm	6.5–9 mm	9–15 mm	15 mm and larger
Recommended Hook in U.S. Size Range	Steel 6, 7, 8*** Regular hook B–1	B–1 to E–4	E–4 to 7	7 to I–9	I–9 to K–10½	K–10½ to M–13	M–13 to Q	Q and larger

   * GUIDELINES ONLY: The above reflect the most commonly used gauges and needle or hook sizes for specific yarn categories.

  ** Lace weight yarns are usually knitted or crocheted on larger needles and hooks to create lacy, openwork patterns. Accordingly, a gauge range is difficult to determine. Always follow the gauge stated in your pattern.

*** Steel crochet hooks are sized differently from regular hooks—the higher the number, the smaller the hook, which is the reverse of regular hook sizing.

*Source: Craft Yarn Council of America's **www.YarnStandards.com***

Notes on the Instructions

- When a number appears before the stitch name, such as 3 dc, work these stitches into the same stitch—for example, "3 dc into the next st."
- When only one stitch is to be worked into each of a number of stitches, it can be written like this: "1 sc in each of next 3 sts." When a number appears after a chain—for example, "ch 10"—this means you should work the number of chains indicated.
- The asterisks mark a specific set of instructions that is repeated—for example, "* 2 sc in next st, 1 dc in next st, rep from * across" means repeat the stitches from the asterisk to next given instruction.
- When instructions are given with parenthesis, it can mean three things. For example, "(2 dc, ch 1, 2 dc) in the next st" means work 2 dc, ch 1, 2 dc all into the same stitch. It can also mean that a set of stitches is repeated a number of times—for example, "(sc in next st, 2 sc in next st) 6 times." Last, the number(s) given at the end of a row or round in parentheses denote(s) the number of stitches or spaces you should have on that row or round.
- A few of the patterns include stitch tutorials, which you'll find under "Special Stitches." In most cases these stitches are specific to that specific pattern.
- Be sure to read the "Pattern Notes" section before beginning a project. You'll find helpful hints there, and the notes will often clear up any questions about the project.

Stitch Guide

Slipknot

This adjustable knot will begin every crochet project.

1. Make a loop in the yarn.

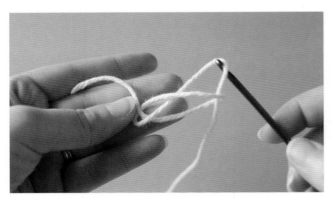

2. With crochet hook or finger, grab the yarn from the skein and pull through loop.

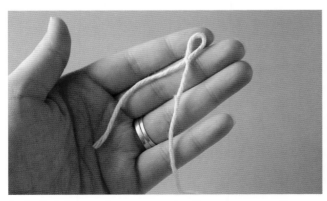

3. Pull tight on the yarn and adjust to create the first loop.

Chain (ch)

The chain provides the foundation for your stitches at the beginning of a pattern. It also can serve as a stitch within a pattern and can be used to create an open effect.

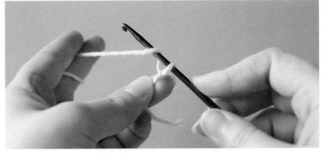

1. Insert hook through the slip knot and place the yarn over the hook by passing the hook in front of the yarn.

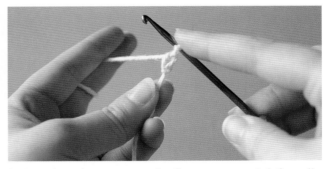

2. Keeping the yarn taught (but not too tight), pull the hook back through the loop with the yarn. Ch 1 is complete.

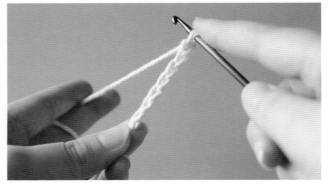

3. Repeat Steps 1 and 2 to create multiple chains.

Slip Stitch (sl st)

The slip stitch is used to join one stitch to another or to join a stitch to another point. It can also be used within the pattern as a stitch without height.

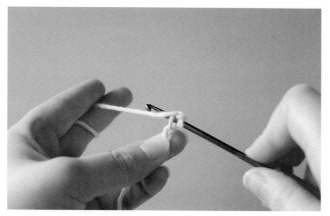

1. Insert the hook from the front of the stitch to the back of the stitch and yarn over; join as for a chain stitch.

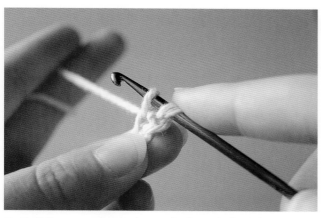

2. Pull the yarn back through the stitch: 2 loops on hook.

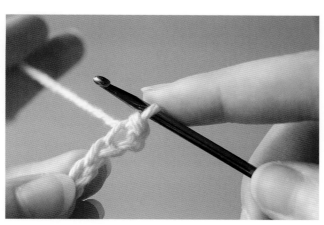

3. Continue to pull the loop through the first loop on the hook to finish.

Single Crochet (sc)

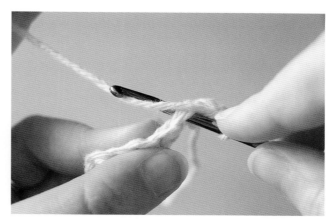

1. Insert hook from the front of the stitch to the back and yarn over.

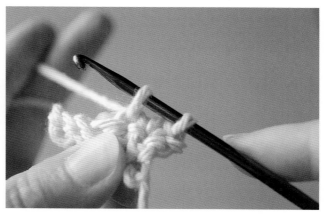

2. Pull the yarn back through the stitch: 2 loops on hook.

3. Yarn over and draw through both loops on the hook to complete.

Back Loop and Front Loop

At times you will be instructed to work in the front loop only (flo) or the back loop only (blo) of a stitch to create a texture within the pattern.

Inserting hook to crochet into the front loop only (flo) of a stitch.

Inserting hook to crochet into the back loop only (blo) of a stitch.

Unless specified otherwise, you will insert your hook under both loops to crochet any stitch.

Half Double Crochet (hdc)

1. Yarn over and insert hook from the front of the stitch to the back.

2. Yarn over and pull yarn back through stitch: 3 loops on hook.

3. Yarn over and draw through all 3 loops on hook to complete.

Double Crochet (dc)

1. Yarn over and insert the hook from the front of the stitch to the back.

2. Yarn over and pull the yarn back through the stitch: 3 loops on hook.

3. Yarn over and draw the yarn through the first 2 loops on the hook: 2 loops on hook.

4. Yarn over and draw the yarn through the last 2 loops on the hook to complete.

Treble Crochet (tr)

1. Yarn over 2 times and insert the hook from the front of the stitch to the back. Yarn over and pull the yarn back through the stitch: 4 loops on hook.

2. To complete: (Yarn over and draw the yarn through the first 2 loops on the hook) 3 times.

Single Crochet 2 Together (sc2tog)

A single crochet 2 together (also known as a decrease) will take 2 stitches and make them into 1 single crochet stitch.

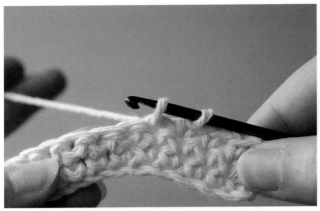

1. Insert the hook from the front of the stitch to the back and yarn over. Pull the yarn back through the stitch: 2 loops on hook.

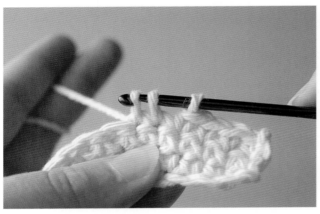

2. Leaving the loops on the hook, insert the hook front to back in the next stitch. Yarn over and pull back through stitch: 3 loops on hook.

3. Yarn over and draw through all 3 loops on the hook to complete.

Double Crochet 2 Together (dc2tog)

A double crochet will take 2 stitches and make them into 1 double crochet stitch.

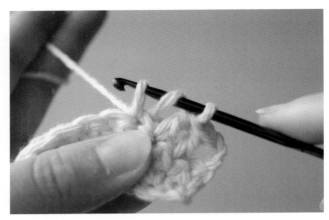

1. Yarn over and insert the hook from the front of the stitch to the back. Yarn over and pull the yarn back through the stitch: 3 loops on hook.

2. Yarn over and draw the yarn through the first 2 loops on the hook: 2 loops on hook.

3. Leaving the loops on the hook, insert the hook from front to back into the next stitch. Yarn over and pull back through the stitch: 4 loops on hook.

4. Yarn over and draw the yarn through the first 2 loops on the hook: 3 loops on hook.

5. Yarn over and draw the yarn through all 3 loops on the hook to complete.

Working on the Post of the Stitch

Each stitch has a post. When working a front post stitch or back post stitch, use the post instead of the top stitch. This is the dc post.

Front Post Double Crochet (FPdc)

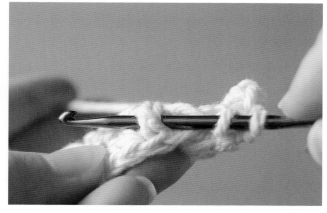

1. Yarn over, insert the hook from the front to the back to the front around the post of the stitch.

2. Yarn over and pull the yarn back around the post: 3 loops on hook.

3. Complete like a double crochet: Yarn over and draw the yarn through the first 2 loops on the hook: 2 loops on hook. Yarn over and draw the yarn through the last 2 loops on the hook to complete.

To work the Back Post Double Crochet (BPdc), simply work from back to front to back around the post and complete steps 2 and 3 from Front Post Double Crochet.

Color Change
When changing colors, use this technique.

1. Complete your given stitch until the last pull through.

2. Yarn over the next color and pull through to finish the stitch and color change. Cut or drop the yarn from the original color.

Stitch Abbreviations

beg	begin/begins/beginning
blo	back loop only
BPdc	back post double crochet
BPsc	back post single crochet
ch(s)	chain/chains
ch-	refers to chain or space previously made
ch sp(s)	chain spaces(s)
cl(s)	cluster(s)
cm	centimeters
dc	double crochet
dc2tog	double crochet 2 stitches together
dc3tog	double crochet 3 stitches together
dec	decrease
flo	font loop only
FPdc	front post double crochet
FPsc	front post single crochet
g	gram(s)
hdc	half double crochet
hdc2tog	half double crochet 2 stitches together
inc	increase
mm	millimeter
oz.	ounce(s)
rem	remaining
rep(s)	repeat(s)
rnd(s)	round(s)
RS	right side
sc	single crochet
sc2tog	single crochet 2 stitches together
sk	skip
sl st(s)	slip stitch(es)
sp(s)	space(s)
st(s)	stitch(es)
tog	together
tr	treble
WS	wrong side
yd.	yard(s)

Acknowledgments

The finished items were photographed by Jennifer Payne, owner of Backroad Photography by Jenn, in her awesome studio in Snead, Alabama. Her creative work has brought all of these items to life!

None of the items could have been crocheted without the stunning yarn. I would like to thank Red Heart, Knit Picks, Lion Brand Yarns, Plymouth Yarn, Premier Yarns, Cascade Yarns, and Patons for their generous support of this book.

Also, thanks to my stitch assistants Tabatha Widner and Danielle Wooley. Much obliged for your hard work!

Last (but not least), I would like to thank my family. Their love and support drive me to make each item cuter than the next. You're my inspiration and heart. Thanks, Jason, my amazing husband, for working with me hand in hand every day. I love you all!

Visual Index

Little Slugger
Blanket   2

Cozy Panda Hat   6

Twinkles Tunic   10

Baby's First Dino   14

Itty-Bitty Britches   18

Sweetums Circle
Vest   22

Baby Shark Hooded
Blanket   26

Blossom Bib   30

Sprinkle Socks   34

Limelight Newborn
Hat   38

Limelight No-Scratch
Mittens   42

Under the Sea
Mobile   44

Sweet Dreams
Sleepsack   48

Sweetcakes Stacker
Rings   52

Cutie-Pie Stitch
Sampler Blanket   56

Spun Sugar
Bonnet   60

Birdie Lovie   64

Swaddle Cocoon   68

Cuddle Me Stroller
Blanket   72

Wiggle Bum Diaper
Cover and Headband
Set   76

Dazzle Beanie   80

Snuggle Bunny   84

Lil' Boss Pullover   88

Chickie Leg
Warmers   92

Roly-Poly Play
Mat   96

Baby Burp Cloth and
Bottle Cozy   100

Hopscotch Baby
Booties   104

Doodlebug
Capris   108

Giggles the Owl
Pillow   112

Bubba Baby
Vest   116

Button Up
Sweater   120

Cupcake Toy   126

Sweetpea
Topper   130

Baby Mat   134

Jelly Bean Car Seat
Cover   138

Lovey-Dovey
Blanket   142

Darling Daisy
Vest   146

Big Champ Hooded
Jacket   150

Half-Pint
Loafers   156

Precious Princess
Slippers   160